Intercultural Negotiation

A guide to preparing, conducting and closing an international negotiation

Manoëlla WILBAUT

Copyright © Dunod, Paris, 2010

All rights reserved. No part of this publication may be reproduced, stored in a retrieval system, or transmitted in any form or by any means, electronic, mechanical, photocopying, recording, or otherwise without the prior permission of the publishers.

Translated from the book *"La négociation interculturelle"*
first published in France by Dunod Éditeur SA in 2010

This English translation first published in 2012 by Management Books 2000 Ltd
Forge House, Limes Road
Kemble, Cirencester
Gloucestershire, GL7 6AD, UK
Tel: 0044 (0) 1285 771441
Fax: 0044 (0) 1285 771055
Email: info@mb2000.com
Web: www.mb2000.com

This book is sold subject to the condition that it shall not, by way of trade or otherwise, be lent, resold, hired out, or otherwise circulated without the publisher's prior consent in any form of binding or cover other than that in which it is published and without a similar condition including this condition being imposed upon the subsequent purchaser.

British Library Cataloguing in Publication Data is available

ISBN 9781852526948

The difference between people around the world is not their origin, their religion, their education, etc. But it is how they see life and what they do with it. So, in essence the people you negotiate or interact with, have aspirations and objectives very similar to your own most often. The art of dealing well with other people then becomes to really understand what they want to achieve and what their own goals are. If you can master the skill to understand the real objectives of people, independent of culture, you have won half the negotiation already. This book will help you beyond this and give you the tools to win the other half of the negotiation.

Boudewijn Arts, Partner Egon Zehnder International

Negotiation implies that there are common interests but also some potential disagreements in determining a working agreement, a contract… It has never been an easy task. However, negotiating with parties that have different cultural backgrounds and expectations can even be more challenging. If things do not happen in the appropriate way, the potential and real costs can reach huge amounts. In major corporations, we can even talk of millions and billions over time! If anyone spends any length of time in a foreign culture, the extent of differences in perceptions, values, priorities… becomes increasingly clear. It is therefore key to have a systematic and structured approach for negotiation. But this approach requires flexibility in the mind because culture and cross cultural differences can be seen in a variety of human interactions where knowledgeable and open minded people make the difference… and reach their negotiation objectives in the most effective way and strong value creation. This is what this book is about and that can make a major difference not only in your professional life but also personally in a world where international interactions keep growing!

Fathi TLATLI, President Global Sector, DHL Customer Solutions and Innovation

In a fast changing multicultural environment such as the one we are currently evolving in, a pragmatic framework is often lacking among executives. How many of us believe their business approach, their empathy, their sensitivity is strong enough to connect with any culture and understanding around the world? Although businessmen conceive there could be differences in theory, in practice everybody has a tendency to reproduce the same approach and behaviour no matter who is the interlocutor. Why? Probably due to a lack of awareness of our own culture impact on the way we are. This book of Manoella Wilbaut has the advantage to provide a pragmatic guideline to understand the behaviour of people from other cultures, but as well, allows each reader to measure the impact of the environment where he/she was raised in on him/her. The outcome is simply a toolbox to enhance the executive management in global business and more simply, a step forward on the path of our personal development.

Clement QUESSETTE, Program Advisor – Executive Education
INSEAD - The Business School for the World®

In international contacts there are differences at the personal and organizational level, in which small details can have a big impact on the outcome. Very often the persons involved will not be aware of the influence of their unconscious frame of mind, and this includes how they deal with intercultural differences. When it comes to negotiations this applies even more, and the pressure of the situation makes people think and act even more rigidly. The standard academic management models will often not work in international settings because they do not incorporate the intercultural factor. In a world where globalization and volatility determine the course of events it is important to dig deeper and understand this. It is precisely the knowledge of the intercultural aspects and how to deal with these that will create the opportunity to build better relationships and obtain better and longer lasting outcomes for all involved. The ideas outlined by Manoella Wilbaut are an enrichment for the reader, and this book should be part of the toolkit for every person involved in international business or politics.

Philippe DEMOULIN, General Manager, Lillo Port Centre (Antwerp, Belgium)

For a complete list of Management Books 2000 titles

visit our web-site at http://www.mb2000.com

To Christine for her invaluable help on this project, as well as so many others.

To Charlie and Elisa for their lovable and inspiring presence.

To Pascale, for the entrepreneurship mindset she has transmitted to me.

CONTENTS

Introduction 13

PART I. Introduction to Intercultural Negotiation 17

Chapter 1. The meaning of culture 21
    What is culture? 21
    The iceberg theory 22
    The levels of culture 23
    The impacts of culture 24
    Ethnocentric traps 26
    Management of cultural differences 27
    Conclusion 28

Chapter 2. Intercultural GPS, a tool to analyse cultures 29
    Intercultural GPS, an analytical model 29
        Point 1 : Relation to time 31
        Point 2 : Rules, values and value orientation 32
        Point 3 : Relation to the individual, actions and decisions 33
        Point 4 : Relation to space and territory 33
        Point 5 : Organisation 34
        Point 6 : Activity 36
        Point 7 : Relation to uncertainty 36
        Point 8 : Reflection modes 36
        Point 9: Communication and relation patterns 37
    Using the intercultural GPS to determine a profile 38
        General questionnaire to decipher a culture 39
        Business questionnaire to decipher a culture 45
    Elements to be taken into consideration when using the intercultural GPS in the framework of negotiations 46
        Avoid the oversimplified binary approach 46
        Avoid confusion between culture, ideology and personality 46
        Assessing culture 46
    Conclusion 49

PART 2. Intercultural negotiation method 51
    The SNA method in brief 52
    The SNA method seen from an intercultural perspective 54
        Identifying the fundamental variables of negotiation 54
        Identifying the impact of culture on these variables 56

Chapter 3. The keys to a successful intercultural negotiation 59
Make sure the balance of power is favourable to you 59
    The levers of power and how to use them 60
    List of key tactics enabling to influence the balance of power 62
Case studies 69
Managing the negotiation climate 71
    Time 71
    Space 73
    Mood 75
    Importance of trust and self-esteem 76
Case studies 77
Managing the negotiation stages 80
Case Studies 84
Remaining in the negotiation zone 86
    Proactively consider a fallback option – BATNA/MESORE 87
    Breaking the deadlock 88
Case studies 92
Adapting the language used 93
    Communication model 93
Case studies 94
Using the power of listening and asking questions 96
    Active listening 97
    The power of asking questions 98
    The importance of answers 100
    The power of silence 101
Case studies 102
Conclusion 103

Chapter 4. How to prepare the negotiation 105
How to establish contacts in business 105
Case studies 106
Identifying the parties to the negotiation 107
    Tool: the influence matrix 109
Case studies 110
Identifying the negotiators' objectives, determining the negotiation threshold and finding common ground 116
    Definition of the objectives 116
    Classification of the objectives 116
    The negotiation threshold 117
    Finding common ground 118
Case studies 120
Identifying what influences and motivates parties 122
    Tool: CASEPriN 122
Case studies 123

Analyzing the situation 124
    Cost/impact or cost/risk matrix 124
    Stakes analysis matrix 127
Case studies 131
Choosing a negotiating style, identifying the other parties' style and choosing a negotiation strategy 132
    Classification of negotiating styles 133
    Choice of a negotiating style 134
    Strategic use of trump cards 136
    Weiss' model of culturally responsive strategies 136
    Strategic choice of the number of negotiators 137
Case studies 138
Organising the meeting and interactions 142
    Identifying practices in terms of protocol and communication 142
    Identifying entertainment habits 142
Case studies 145
Conclusion 153

Chapter 5. How to conduct the negotiation 155
Starting the negotiation 156
    Intercultural aspect of visual contacts 156
    Intercultural aspect of the notion of personal and public space 157
Case studies 157
Clarifying the real requests of the other party 160
    How can you determine the real request? 161
Case studies 162
Managing group dynamics 163
Case studies 164
Making proposals 165
Case studies 167
Making progress in the negotiation 168
    How to make progress in the negotiation according to the type of company you are in 168
Case studies 171
Responding to the other party's proposals and reactions 173
    Some tactics to save time 174
    Responding to the other party's reactions 174
    Avoiding emotional reactions 176
Case studies 178
Taking a stand 179
Case studies 180
Conclusion 180

Chapter 6. How to close the negotiation plan for the future 181
  Concluding the negotiation by yourself 182
  Case studies 182
  Starting the conclusion 183
  Case studies 186
  Making your final offer and overcoming the possible reluctance of the other parties 186
    Making your final offer 186
    Encouraging the other party to close the negotiation 187
  Case studies 189
  Concluding the negotiation with the support of one or more third parties 189
    Calling upon a third party 190
  Implementing decisions 191
  Case studies 192
  Considering future prospects 194
  Case studies 194
  Conclusion 195

PART 3. Self-assessment and putting theory into practice 197

Chapter 7. Assessment of your negotiating style and skills 199
  Characteristics and skills of an experienced
  international negotiator 199
  Assessing your negotiating skills and style 200
    Assessing your negotiating skills 200
    Assessing your negotiating style 201
  Conclusion 206

Chapter 8. Integration scenario 207
  Case study: 207
  Establishment of an industrial consortium with the support of the European Community 207
    General context 207
    Preparation of the negotiation 212
    Conducting the negotiation 216

Chapter 9. Practical forms for use during negotiations 225
  Form for the preparation of a negotiation 225
  Form for the conduct of the negotiation 229
  Form for the closing of the negotiation and future prospects 230
  Form to be used throughout the negotiation 231

Bibliography 233
Index of Ideas 237
Index of Countries 239

PREFACE

Many people associate negotiation with conflict management or even with contract dealings. This book invites the readerto have a broader perspective and to go well beyond these interesting but more resticted topics! "How are we to establish long-term partnerships?" "How can we become vectors of constructive change and development?" These are the most essential questions.

Over the last 200 years or so, we have witnessed significant changes in the commercial environment: the globalisation of trade (in some respects, the world has become a village), the advent of speed for speed's sake, the increased momentum of the acceleration mode in which we live (made possible through the development of new information technologies), the emergence of short-termism (which goes along with obvious malfunctions in businesses and in financial markets). In negotiation, it is essential to take these factors into account! Many of us have the feeling of riding on a fast, winding and blurred trackwhich we did not exactly choose. In the 21st Century, there is a clear return to the search for long-term meaning. **Going fast, of course, but going where?**

Is the search for meaning the business of all? We often hear it said "this is modern society, we can't do anything about it". Om the contrary, it is the responsibility of the group (as as of every single individual) to act in the most sensible and responsible way to get the racing car (and all its passengers) to the right destination and in the best possible condition.Thinking we can control everything is an illusion, but it is essential for everybody to carefully consider every situation. "One-man shows" are a thing of the past.

Today's winners, and most notably those of tomorrow, will be the one who manage, with cleverness and respect, to capitalise on human networks and on the environment's resources (material or not), wherever they may be (Asia, Europe, South and North America, Africa, the Middle-East...).

What is the place of intercultural negotiation in this context? Intercultural negotiation is considered as a meaningful tool helping (if there is such a willingness from the parties) to win together on a long-term basis rather than simply winning "one against the other" on a short-term basis. On the international stage, there are more misunderstandings than deep disagreements. And of course, the higher the stakes, the stronger the reactions. What is happening underneath the surface? What's in the black box? Having a modular approach and adapted tools to analyze the situation and react quickly and effectively for better and long-term results is certainly helpful!

Dear readers, I invite you to go beyaond appearances to constantly learn from others, to push back the boundaries, to be more ambitious and innovative and, most importantly, to go further together...

Manoëlla Wilbaut

"We must free ourselves of the hope that the sea will ever rest. We must learn to sail in high winds."
Aristotle Onassis

INTRODUCTION

Entering the world of negotiation is a surprising adventure. Negotiation is connected with the most complex and emotionally-charged human relations. It links up with the notions of power-play, status, distribution of resources ...

Several questions arise:
- how should we interact in order to achieve our goals?
- which paths will be followed and which of them will be knowingly avoided?
- how is the notion of negotiation itself perceived?

It is interesting to notice how different can be the views of various individuals on the same situation. We do not see the world through the same eyes, through the same system of references... All our senses are influenced by our broader experiences. Our expectations, our deep-seated motives are, amongst others, influenced by our environment.

These differences are even more visible and remarkable in interactions involving people from different cultures. The outlines are drawn and the contrasts become apparent when people from different horizons meet.

People working on the international stage are not the only ones exposed to these cultural differences. In the present world, we all are intercultural players: at school, at work, in political institutions or in associations...

Managing contacts between different cultures is a major challenge. These cultural differences are priceless for those who can grasp them. Capitalising on these differences, instead of being affected by them, enables individuals to distinguish themselves on the long run. This constitutes a critical competitive advantage, whatever the sphere of activity considered.

The intercultural aspect is, and shall remain for many decades, a topical subject. Its relevance is constantly growing alongside the increase of global exchanges.

In order to efficiently grasp intercultural contacts, it is necessary to have an effective reading tool. The intercultural GPS is a modular tool which allows to unravel and understand the essence and bases of cultures. For the purpose of this book, the intercultural GPS has been combined with a practical negotiating method enabling readers to put understanding into practice!

Structure and use of the book

The first part of this book establishes the framework. The purpose is to enable the reader to understand the foundations of intercultural negotiation and the meaning of culture as well as to decode cultures by means of a practical and innovative tool: the intercultural GPS.

The second part puts forward an effective negotiation method, which can be activated immediately: the SNA (Successful Negotiation Activator). This method is presented in a logical order. The tools that can be employed in order to open, conduct and close a negotiation are successively presented. Before "entering" this process, the reader is invited to consider the keys to a successful intercultural negotiation. These are principles that should be respected throughout the negotiation process. It is the breeding ground for successful negotiations, the bond without which the negotiating party cannot expose the whole of his potential. This part is full of examples linking together the Intercultural GPS and the SNA method.

The third part is about putting theory into practice and self-assessment. The reader is invited to assess his/her style and competences in order to act accordingly. An integration scenario offers a useful overview.

Chapter 9 includes several forms to be used during the preparation of the negotiation, during its conduct and conclusion or even throughout the whole process.

The book includes many examples relating to the countries presented in table 1.

Table 1 – Countries illustrated in this book

	Country	Code		Country	Code		Country	Code
	Argentina	AR		Germany	DE		Saudia Arabia	SA
	Australia	AU		India	IN		South Africa	ZA
	Austria	AT		Indonesia	ID		Spain	ES
	Belgium	BE		Italy	IT		Sweden	SE
	Brazil	BR		Japan	JP		Thailand	TH
	Canada	CA		Mexico	MX		Tunisia	TN
	China	CH		Morocco	MA		Turkey	TR
	Cuba	CU		Poland	PL		Ukraine	UA
	Egypt	EG		Romania	RO		United Kingdom	UK
	France	FR		Russia	RU		United States	US

Who is this book intended for and what does it provide?

Reader's profile

This book is intended for all negotiators, whatever their level of experience. Its modular structure allows the reader to concentrate on specific aspects of the method he/she wishes to go more thoroughly into.

Expected results

The book's aim is to enable those working on the international stage (and the other intercultural players) to acquire, in a few weeks only, strong skills in intercultural negotiation in order to positively distinguish themselves on the long run.

PART I

INTRODUCTION TO INTERCULTURAL NEGOTIATION

"Buying is cheaper than asking."
German saying

According to the common feeling that intercultural negotiation is a "sub-branch" of negotiation in general. In reality, the opposite is rather the case. Negotiating on the international stage proves more complex than doing so in a culturally "uniform" environment. Therefore, in order to grasp intercultural negotiation, it is necessary to simultaneously integrate the concepts of negotiation and culture.

Let us start by considering what negotiation is

Negotiation is the process through which two or more interlocutors try to reach an agreement together. This endeavour is limited in time, based on quantifiable issues and implies the confrontation of diverging interests.

In theory, *intercultural negotiation* takes place when the participating parties come from different cultures. The same goes for *international negotiation*, "between nations". In practice, the choice of terminology often depends on the circumstances: intercultural (when one wishes to underline the intercultural dimension) or international (when one wishes to underline the international aspects). Let us take the example of a French tourist negotiating the price of a djembe in Senegal. In that case, we would rather refer to intercultural negotiation.

Negotiations can be classified according to the number of parties involved (bilateral or multilateral), according to the level of interaction (by mutual agreement[1] or via an organised market[2]) or even according to the object of the negotiation (juridical, legal, commercial).

There are four prerequisites for negotiation:

1. Recognising that exchange is founded on compromise and cooperation: without these, negotiating would not be possible. One of the secrets of successful negotiations is to understand that each concession must be compensated by an advantage. In terms of concessions, it is necessary to draw a distinction between those which are acceptable and those which are not. Beyond concessions, cooperation is usually the only way to create win-win situations.
2. Being willing to understand the needs and operation methods of the

---

1   In negotiation by mutual agreement (OTC), the parties know each other and are legally bound to one another. However, the negotiation can take place through a broker, but his role is limited to putting the parties in contact with each other. On this kind of unofficial market, all the terms of the contract can be negotiated, as long as the parties reach an agreement. It is a "tailor-made" market.
2   In an organised market, the parties are not acquainted with each other. All operations are concluded through a single mediator, responsible for the appropriate conclusion of the contracts: the clearing house. The contracts aare standardised and prices depend on the law of supply and demand

negotiating parties: it is essential to understand what is behind their actions and reactions. Along the same lines, we should also identify our own operation methods. Keeping these facts in mind makes the process of negotiation easier. Without the willingness to understand the parties' needs, the final outcome of negotiation will always be uncertain. In negotiations, one has to distinguish the contents from the container. It is also necessary to make a distinction between three elements: the actual content of the negotiation, the process and the negotiating parties.

3. Having one or several common interests: the negotiating parties must share a common interest. It is recommended to make sure that this common goal is obvious to everyone.
4. Having free will: negotiation is only possible when the parties are free to make their own choices.

Let us now consider the typical negotiation process.

The vast majority of negotiations, whether they be intercultural or not, follow a similar pattern made up of six successive stages: the preparation stage, the introduction stage, the differentiation stage, the integration stage, the decision stage and the follow-up stage.

The negotiation process which is introduced in this book is an adaptation of the process described by Graham (figure 1).

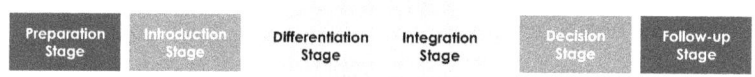

Figure I.1. Graham's negotiation process
(adapted by Manoëlla Wilbaut)

– *Preparation stage:* information gathering. At this stage, the parties identify the potential problems to be debated and to be given priority. In case of group negotiation, it is recommended to meet as a team before the introduction stage in order to establish an agreement on several points, such as the internal communication code of the team, the subjects to be developed…
– *Introduction stage:* setting up. The parties set the scene and try to forge relations by seeking common ground.

- *Differentiation stage:* analysing all types of divergences and examining views from different perspectives. The parties look into their differences, take a stand and determine the boundaries of the "conflict area".
- *Integration stage:* returning to common ground and underlining the points of agreement. The parties seek alternative solutions that might be used to solve problems and reach an agreement. At this stage, the points on which the parties agree are obvious.
- *Decision stage:* agreement. The parties make the final offer and seal the agreement.
- *Follow-up stage:* the basic negotiation process ends here. On the other hand, in a majority of cases, a seasoned negotiator will see to the follow-up of the negotiation and keep working on relations for the future.

Seasoned negotiators are familiar with these stages and prepare themselves for each one of them. They also take various decisions depending on the evolution of the negotiation: choice of the best time to introduce some strategies, make concessions and formulate a final offer... Finally, they know that in order to achieve an optimal result, each stage must be developed fully and without haste.

Negotiation is a purely *human* activity. Men negotiate to get material goods (such as consumer goods) or even to get less tangible elements (such as prestige or recognition). Men also negotiate in order to communicate and exchange. For example, in the United States, negotiation is mainly of functional nature. In other parts of the world, such as the Middle-East, it also has a social purpose. The cultural context has a strong influence on the notion of negotiation itself.

While negotiation is a long-standing activity which has been used for several thousand years old, we must consider it in its present context. Global exchanges are constantly growing and intercultural contacts are part of our daily lives. *Taking intercultural aspects into account is not an option anymore. Nowadays, it is a necessity!*

CHAPTER 1

THE MEANING OF CULTURE

"Culture hides much more than it reveals, and strangely enough what it hides, it hides most effectively from its own participants.
Edward Hall

Subject: understanding the essence, basis and impacts of culture, but also distinguishing what is cultural from what is not.

Culture is said to be omnipresent. The concept was lightly touched upon, but what does culture it exactly mean? This chapter contemplates the notion of culture from every angle:

- what are the characteristics of culture?
- what are the different components and aspects of culture?
- how does culture manifest itself?
- what are the ethnocentric traps?
- etc.

What is culture?

Culture is an integrated system of behavioural patterns specific to the members of a society. It is also a common system of definitions enabling its members to provide automatic solutions to recurrent problems. Anything the group thinks, says and does belongs to the field of culture.

Culture is transmitted, stable, forgotten, functional, based on values, long-term oriented, of arbitrary nature and it satisfies the needs of people within a society.

Culture is transmitted through language, beliefs and traditions. Culture is thus acquired and not genetically transmissible. Though in constant evolution, one could say that culture is stable. It is also true that culture is "forgotten" as individuals tend to loose sight of the fact that it is the result of acquired behaviours. Most people only realise their cultural specificities when in contact with people from different cultures. Elements that are invisible within a same culture become visible by an effect of contrast.

Culture has a functional purpose as it provides the main behavioural orientations of a group, which is crucial for its survival. Being a social phenomenon, culture is based on values. It makes communication within the group easier. Moreover, culture is long-term oriented. Cultural practices are arbitrary in nature, as behaviours considered acceptable in one culture are not considered the same way in other cultures. Present-day cultures are the result of accumulation of experiences and knowledge several thousand years old. Finally, culture satisfies the needs of people in a society. In this manner, depending on the evolution of a society's needs, culture develops new features and discards practices and ways of thinking.

The iceberg theory

The iceberg theory underlines the fact that the physical demonstrations of culture (such has people's behaviours, their language, the know-how they develop and the institutions they rely on) merely reflect the foundations of their culture.

The foundations of a given culture are shared assumptions, rules and values. These elements are not visible and can only be inferred, which makes them more difficult to grasp. According to the iceberg theory, the foundations are the base of the physical demonstrations of culture, so it is important to identify them.

Going beyond the sphere of what is visible is trying to understand the reasons and to gain more influence upon them (figure 1.1)!

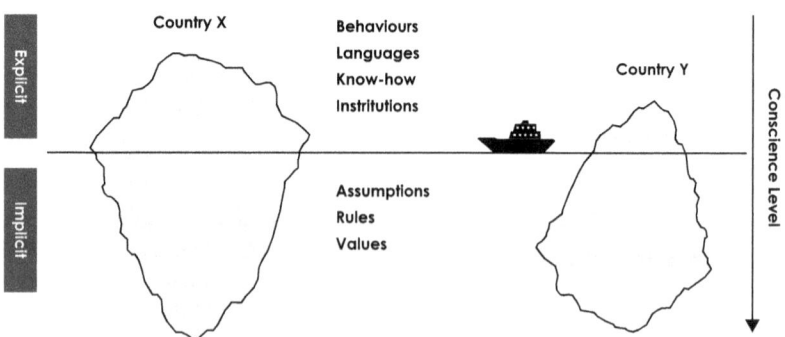

Figure 1.1 – The iceberg theory

- Through culture groups share common *assumptions/suppositions* about the means of external adaptation or internal integration considered the most appropriate.
- *Rules* are collective definitions of what is considered appropriate or not by the group.
- *Values* are the less visible elements of culture. They are at its core. They correspond to the broader preferences of the group and very strong emotions are attached to them. Values refer to what is good or bad, beautiful or ugly, desirable or not. These values are accompanied by internal "sanctions" of various degrees.

By visible elements of culture we mean:
- *behaviours:* customs and traditions in all areas of human activity, such as medicine, hygiene, management, clothing, diet, housing...;
- *languages:* verbal and non-verbal;
- *know-how:* communication codes, artistic techniques, scientific knowledge;
- *institutions:* collective ways of organising – family, education system, business, government, religion, justice.

The levels of culture

Being now acquainted with the notion of culture does not mean we should not go further. The concept of culture is multifaceted. There are different levels of culture influencing organisation and evolving through it. (figure 1.2) Each aspect considered should be placed into context. For this reason, in the case of project management, for example, it is recommended not only to proceed to an analysis of the organisational culture, but also to identify the major impacts of the other levels of culture.

Figure 1.2 indicates five levels of culture based on various criteria. These criteria are not definitive and can be adapted on a case-by-case basis.

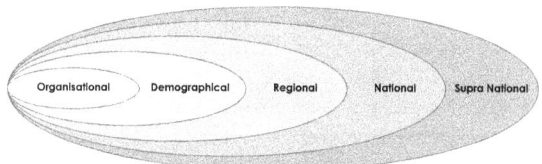

Figure 1.2 – Levels of culture diagrams

While culture is a major element, it cannot account for everything. We should also take into account the interlocutors' personality and the prevailing ideology[3] of the environment in which we find ourselves (figure 1.3).

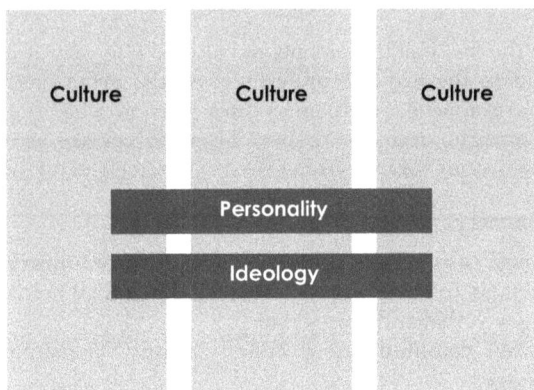

Figure 1.3 – Culture/Personality/ideology matrix

Example : ideology in Cuba versus ideology in China

The government in Cuba disseminates a communist-type ideology, which does not necessarily correspond to a cultural or historical heritage of the country. At first, the spirit was rather entrepreneurial and flexible. The government's ideology is quite far from the local culture and is mainly supported by military force. One could imagine that if that force came to disappear, the communist ideology would not survive.

Like in Cuba, the Chinese government disseminates a communist-type ideology. Nevertheless, we note that this ideology, given its collectivist side, is closer to the Chinese culture. In that sense, the communist ideology is more rooted in the Chinese system than in the Cuban system.

The impacts of culture

Having analyzed culture from different angles, it is obvious that it influences all aspects of our lives in different ways. It has an impact on the way we live, the way we die, the way we organise ourselves and perceive our universe.

---

3   Ideology is a group of systematic beliefs, ideas and dogmas which inflluence individual and collective behaviour. In this analysis it is crucial to define the ideology of a system or the ideology of a group within a system.

From that point, we can deduce all sorts of underlying implications. In part, culture determines how:
- credibility develops: what does credibility given to an individual depend on? His/her age, experience or origin...? Countries with Latin cultures tend to give more attention to the origin and character of an individual than, for example, Anglo-Saxon countries.
- information is conveyed: in low context societies[4], such as in the United States, it is rather easy to get information through written and formal modes (like emails), while in high context societies[5], such as in the Middle-East, people tend to prefer more informal means of communication, like the telephone.
- conflicts are managed: in conflict management, do we use laws and procedures or rather negotiation and mediation? It is observed that in the United States written contracts prevail, whereas in the Middle-East words tend to get the upper hand.
- people communicate: what is the role of words in comparison with implicit elements? The German culture, for example, tends to favour verbal and explicit communication, whereas in Asian cultures the non-verbal and implicit aspects often prevail.
- people exchange and sell things: how do exchanges take place? How long do negotiations last and what is the usual room for manoeuvre? In the Middle-East, we notice that the room for manoeuvre is significant. Bargaining and negotiating are considered as fully-fledged social activities.
- people are assessed: are we assessed on the basis of rather objective or subjective criteria? For example, we notice that in Germany objective criteria prevail.
- etc.

Examples are as informative and unlimited! The list provided is not exhaustive, but gives a good idea of the global situation.

---

[4] The notion of context refers to the way information circulates within a given environment. Depending on the features observed, we can identify whether we are dealing with a low context society or a high context society. In low context cultures, contextual information must be made explicit through an interaction. Usually, people convey information in a much more verbal way and make sure that they are well informed about the topics which affect them and are of interest to them. In these cultures, verbal communication tends to be more important than non-verbal communication (source: Edward T. Hall, Beyond Culture, Paperback, December 7th 1976).

[5] In high context cultures, contextual information is implicit. People in these cultures often transmit more implicit information and have a broader network. Therefore, they tend to remain well informed about many subjects. In these cultures, non-verbal communication is definitely essential.

Ethnocentric traps

When we meet somebody from a different culture, we could be "tempted" to compare ourselves and to interpret the customs and habits of people according to our own criteria. This tendency is called ethnocentrism. Ethnocentrism also makes some people consider that their culture is better than the one of others.

Culture is the expression of a form of adaptation to specific natural environment. All cultures must be assessed in terms of the relevant society. In absolute terms, no culture is superior or inferior to others. Ethnocentric behaviours close doors and restrict the level of understanding. It is essential to avoid at all costs the comparison of cultures. *Cultures are different and these differences do not depend on an order of hierarchy.*

Our relations with groups are often determined by stereotypes[6]. If we want to take a relationship further, it is essential to go beyond stereotypes. Nevertheless, in some cases, stereotypes can have a positive impact. For example, some can be used as a stepping stone in order to get more information about a group at a later stage. Useful stereotypes have one or more of the following characteristics:
 - consciously remembered (group rule);
 - descriptive rather than evaluative (i.e. neither good nor bad);
 - precise (describe the rule or the group);
 - modified (based on additional observations).

The three main ethnocentric traps are the following:
 - ignoring differences;
 - recognising differences and casting a negative judgment upon them;
 - recognising differences while playing down their importance.

It takes discipline to go beyond ethnocentric traps. When an individual is confronted with other cultures, s/he may suffer a cultural shock[7], the intensity of which is proportional to the tendency of interpreting the customs or habits of others according to his/her own culture. In order to fully benefit from what other cultures have to offer, it is necessary to go beyond prejudice.

"Intercultural communication triggers more misunderstandings than disagreements. The problem is that disagreements are much easier to identify than misunderstandings"
H. Lachman, Chairman of Steel Case Straford

---

6   Stereotypes are a form of categorisation organising and defining our behaviour towards various groups in society. Stereotypes never describe individual behaviour perfectly; they rather describe the behavioural rule of a particular group's.

7   A culture shock is an emotional shock triggered when a person or a group wrongly interpret actions of people from different cultures.

Management of cultural differences

There are different ways of managing cultural differences. The possibilities provided below are presented in ascending order, according to their level of cultural integration:
- *recognise and accept differences:* the notion of acceptance is linked to the notion of respect. Cultural differences of different levels are identified and accepted. In practice and without a deeper understanding it may be difficult to accept foreign beliefs and customs.
- *adapt to differences:* the notion of adaptation refers to the notion of empathy. We try to put ourselves in others' shoes. In order to adapt ourselves to another culture, we must abandon our comfort zone and be willing to temporarily adopt different values, rules and assumptions.
- *integrate differences:* the notion of integration goes much further than the notion of adaptation, as it is not only a temporary change. Integration is possible when an individual is able to simultaneously manage several systems of references.
- *capitalise on differences:* the notion of capitalisation is strongly linked to the notion of proactivity. At this stage, the individual tries spontaneously to discover the treasures of his own culture and those of other cultures, while inciting others to follow his example.

The higher the level of cultural integration, the stronger the propensity for positive results (figure 1.4).

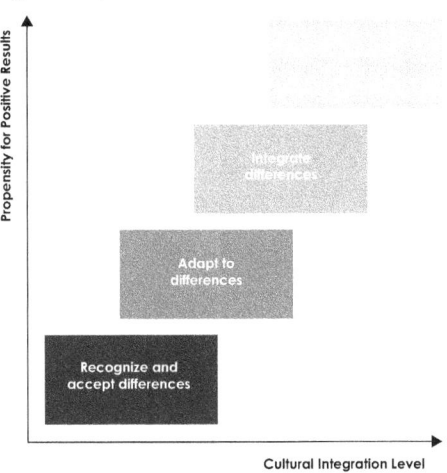

Figure 1.4 - Cultural adaptation matrix

Until not long ago, a school of thought tended to promote the existence of universally valid organisation tools and methods. Nowadays, we realise this trend turned out to be a deadlock. There are no universal answers, only solutions to specific problems.

This book advocates – like thousands of economists, politicians, entrepreneurs, journalists and other enlightened contributors from around the world – a "glocal" approach of negotiation for the business community as well as for the environment, in general.

Having a "glocal" approach in negotiation means having clear global views and objectives, while being able to take into account the cultural specificities of individuals and of negotiating environments (figure 1.5).

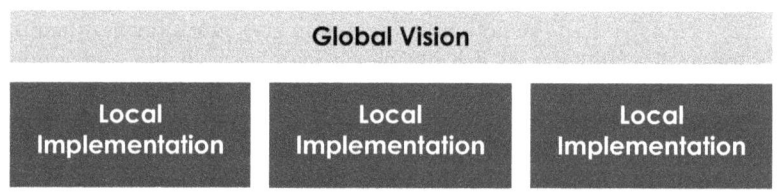

Figure 1.5 – "Glocal" approach

Conclusion

Culture is omnipresent and inherent to all human organisations. Culture consolidates organisations in the following ways:
- uniting the members of a same culture;
- giving a meaning to their lives;
- in a way, making their lives easier by providing a number of predefined answers to given problems;
- culture is multifaceted. It would be vain and counter-productive to try and reduce it to its simplest expression. There are different levels of integration but, generally speaking, the higher the level of integration, the stronger the propensity for positive results. In our increasingly interconnected world, in which exchanges are constantly growing, the ability to capitalise on cultural diversity is definitely a source of competitive advantages.

CHAPTER 2

INTERCULTURAL GPS, A TOOL TO ANALYSE CULTURES

"The flexibility and ability to adapt are essential tools to deal with the most difficult situations."
Anonymous quote

Subject: having a concrete method and tools at one's disposal to identify the features and basic elements of a culture, in order to eventually be able to capitalise on cultural differences.

There are different stages in the intercultural approach:
- at first, spotting the cultural differences;
- then, defining what is behind them;
- later, understanding the whole picture (get a panoramic view rather than a narrow perspective);
- finally, "feeling" these cultural differences in order to capitalise on them.

Capitalising on cultural differences requires a set of guidelines and a powerful lever tool. Gathering facts and anecdotes is entertaining but far from being enough to efficiently grasp diversified multicultural relations. For this reason, this book offers the reader a "smooth-running machine"!

The intercultural GPS is a model allowing to efficiently analyze the culture of an individual or an organisation. Apart from the model, the reader shall also find a practical way of activating this tool, in order to use it in the field of negotiation.

Intercultural GPS, an analytical model

Understanding the existence of cultural differences having an impact on our universe is one thing. Knowing how to identify in concrete terms the foundations and key dynamics of a society is another.

The intercultural GPS, the model developed in this chapter, gives a panoramic view of national and regional cultures. A tool that is comprehensive, pragmatic and ready-to-use at the same time!

Intercultural Negotiation

The points considered are classified under nine areas of analysis (figure 2.1).
1. Relation to time;
2. Rules, values and value orientation;
3. Relation to individuals, actions and decisions;
4. Relation to space and territory;
5. Organisation;
6. Activity;
7. Relation to uncertainty;
8. Reflection modes;
9. Communication and relation patterns.

1. Relation to time	2. Rules, values and value orientation	3. Relation to individuals, actions and decisions
• Monochronic approach vs. Polychronic approach • Past-, present- or future-oriented • Monetary time vs. factual time	• Masculinity versus femininity • Religion, education, aesthetics...	• Pragmatic approach vs. Dogmatic approach • Do ('do-er' attitude) vs. be ('be-er' attitude) – linked to the relation between man and nature • Individualistic approach vs. Collectivistic approach • Beliefs: of natural source vs. of ideological source vs. of relational source vs. of factual source

9. Communication and relation patterns		4. Relation to space and territory
• Predominance of verbal language vs. predominance of non-verbal language • Direct approach vs. indirect approach • formal approach vs. informal approach • High context vs. low context • Specific approach versus generic approach • Neutrality versus emotion/externalization	 **CULTURE**	• Restricted informal space vs. developed informal space • High space value vs. moderate space value • Private approach vs. public approach

8. Reflection modes		5. Organization
• Analytical approach vs. systemic approach • deductive approach vs. inductive approach • Dialogue-oriented vs. data-oriented		• Collaboration-oriented vs. competition-oriented • Stability vs. change • Prevailing managerial logic: contract vs. consensus vs. honour • Universalist approach vs. particularist approach • Significant hierarchical distance (hierarchy) vs. small hierarchical distance (equality)

7. Relation to uncertainty	6. Activity	
• Tolerance for high uncertainty vs. tolerance for low uncertainty	• Consumer patterns • Material culture	

Figure 2.1 – Intercultural GPS (M. Wilbaut)

Point 1 : Relation to time

Defining relation to time provides indications on the way members of an organisation value time, on the way they manage it and on the way they organise their activities in time. In order to define relation to time, we must consider three factors.

▶ The value of time

Is time considered a scarce resource (in that case, we talk of "monetary time") or an abundant resource (or "factual time")?

▶ Time management: monochronism versus polychronism

Within a polychronic approach, members of an organisation manage several activity flows at the same time. Polychronic individuals do not mind being interrupted while they are working. Time commitments are considered as goals to achieve if possible. These people change easily their plans. They usually belong to high context environments and are used to building long-lasting relationships. The notion of private property exists; however, they borrow and lend things very easily. These people strongly value their close relations, i.e. family, friends, close business partners. The notion of privacy is much less clear than in low context societies.

Within a monochronic approach, individuals only manage one flow of activities at a time, on which they often concentrate and they do not like being interrupted. They take time commitments (respect of time schedules, deadlines, etc.) very seriously. These people often stick to pre-defined plans, usually belong to low context environments and are used to establishing short-term relationships with others. Most often, they strongly value all aspects relating to private property. Finally, not bothering others and respecting their privacy is very important to them.

▶ Orientation of the organisation in time: past- versus present- versus future-oriented

When a culture is past-oriented, it attaches importance to traditions, roots, etc. The past justifies and influences the current ways of being and acting. When a culture is rather present-oriented, the present time has an impact on the vision of the world and guides our actions.

In future-oriented cultures, the time to come is important to the extent that it relates to the rest of people's lives. In this perspective, the future is generally perceived as something better or, in any case, more important.

Point 2 : Rules, values and value orientation

Defining the rules, values and value orientation enables us to identify the specific collective representations of a group of individuals. Thanks to that, we can rapidly determine what is considered desirable, undesirable, appropriate or inappropriate in a group.

It is essential to determine whether the values the members of a group adhere to are rather of feminine or masculine nature. In male dominated societies, achievement, performance and acquisition of material goods and power are dominant values.

The concept of "having" takes precedence over the concept of "being". In contrast, quality of life and selflessness are the dominant values in female dominated societies.

Moreover, it is important to look into the values shared through religion, surrounding systems (such as the education system) and to observe the way they are transmitted.

Considering the value orientation enables us to get an overall picture of a culture. The following dimensions refer to dimensions used in the other categories:
- relation between man and nature: controlling nature versus adapting to nature – cf. point 3 "Relation to the individual, actions and decisions";
- relation to beliefs: of natural source versus of ideological source versus of relational source versus of factual source – cf. point 3 "Relation to the individual, actions and decisions";
- relation to others: individualistic approach versus collectivistic approach – cf. point 3 "Relation to the individual, actions and decisions";
- relation to power: significant hierarchical distance (hierarchy) versus low hierarchical distance (equality) – cf. point 5 "Organisation";
- relation to time: Monetary time versus factual time – cf. point 1 "Relation to time";
- relation to rules: universalist approach versus particularist approach – cf. point 5 "organisation";
- relation to activity: do ("do-er" attitude) versus be ("be-er" attitude") – cf. point 3 "Relation to the individual, actions and decisions";
- relation to space: private approach versus public approach – cf. point 4 "Relation to space and territory";
- relation to affects: Neutrality versus emotion/externalisation – cf. point 9 "Communication and relation patterns";

— relation to risk: high tolerance for uncertainty versus low tolerance for uncertainty – cf. point 7 "Relation to uncertainty".

Point 3 : Relation to the individual, actions and decisions

The relation to the individual, actions and decisions goes into the importance of the individual and the way s/he acts having an influence on the world. In order to define this relation, we need to consider the following three points:

▶ **Which is the preferred approach regarding action?**

Pragmatic approach versus *dogmatic approach*: in terms of action, should we rather apply and respect rules or look for specific solutions? In cultures where dogmatism is dominant, applying rules and even dogmas prevails over looking for practical solutions applied to a specific context. On the other hand, in the so-called pragmatic cultures, more emphasis is laid on looking for adapted solutions to specific contexts, which allow individuals to address certain challenges.

"Do-er" attitude versus *"be-er" attitude*: In terms of relation to nature, two basic behaviours are observed: the "do-er" attitude and the "be-er" attitude:

The "do-er" attitude advocates control over nature. Human activity is of great importance as one assumes to be able to control the environment, which is also what people wish. The "be-er" attitude advocates adaptation to nature. Human activity is also considered very important but, in this context, the mission is very different. The concept of harmony is fundamental.

▶ **What is the individual's sphere of activity?**

Individualistic approach versus *collectivistic approach*: members of an organisation where individualism prevails are supposed to look after themselves and their "close" family, while in rather collectivist structures the organisation's members belong to subgroups and communities which are supposed to look after them in exchange for their loyalty.

▶ **What kind of argument has the most impact on the decision-making process?**

What are the most relevant elements used to convince the members of a group? Do these points originate from nature, ideology, relations or facts?

Point 4 : Relation to space and territory

The relation to space and territory refers to the value of space, the relevance of the concept of territory and the way it is used.

▸ The value of space

High space value versus *moderate space value*: Where space value is high, space is considered to be a status indicator and bears a strong social importance. On the other hand, where the value of space is moderate, there is no major social meaning attached to space.

▸ Relevance of the concept of territory

Private approach versus *public approach*: in the private approach, individuals protect themselves by building mental barriers (protecting their feelings and privacy) as well as physical ones (reducing intrusions in their private space). On the other hand, in the public approach, individuals forge deeper and stronger bonds with others by sharing their physical and sentimental territory.

▸ Use of territory

Restricted informal space versus *developed informal space*: when informal space is restricted, the relative proximity of individuals in social interactions is accepted. Conversely, in contexts where the informal space is developed, the relative proximity of individuals in social interactions is neither desired nor desirable. The informal space is often called "personal cocoon". This invisible and vague territory, which escapes our consciousness, triggers strong emotional reactions when somebody enters it.

Hall[8] distinguishes four types of interpersonal distances:
- *intimate distance*: estimated between 15 and 45 cm from the interlocutor. There is no body contact but individuals can join hands. Heat and smell are perceptible;
- *personal distance*: estimated between 45 and 75 cm for intimate individuals, and between 75 and 125 cm for social relations, such as friends;
- *social distance*: estimated between 120 and 210 cm. It is the typical distance in a work environment;
- *public distance*: estimated between 3.6 and 7.5 metres, only for formal contacts. This distance is observed in ceremonies, lectures, etc.

Each culture has its own interpretation of these distances. This point will be further developed later.

Point 5 : Organisation

Organisation refers to the way individuals organise themselves in society and the elements these structures reflect. In order to analyze this point, one must

---

8   Hall E. T., *Beyond Culture*, New York, Anchor, 1976

consider four points: the way success is achieved, the intended objective, the underlying managerial logic and the way power is shared.

▸ **The way success is achieved**

Collaboration-oriented versus *competition-oriented*: competition-oriented individuals wish to progress and achieve success through competitive stimuli. On the other hand, collaboration-oriented individuals wish to progress through mutual respect, sharing and solidarity.

Universalist approach versus *particularist approach*: universalist cultures tend to be strongly based on rules and procedures. Their nature is rather abstract and they usually refute all exceptions that might weaken the power of law. These cultures favour the enforcement of rules and procedures in order to guarantee a coherent and fair system. On the other hand, particularist cultures attach more importance to flexibility and adaptation to local situations.

▸ **Intended objective**

Stability versus *change*: when priority is given to stability, static environments are developed. In this case, we observe the implementation of systematic and disciplined approaches and the pursue of efficiency. The rule is to minimise as much as possible changes and ambiguities. On the other hand, when change is favoured, more emphasis is laid on dynamic and flexible environments. We observe the use of innovation and adaptability- based approaches and that efficiency is pursued. The rule is to avoid routine, which is considered as annoying.

▸ **Underlying managerial logic**

Prevailing managerial logic: *contract* versus *consensus* versus *honour*: managerial logic refers to how and why decisions are taken and implemented. When the notion of contract prevails, the parties do business together because they have signed an agreement. When the notion of consensus prevails, apart from interpersonal agreements, the approval, or at least the participation, of the group is necessary. Finally, when the notion of honour prevails, a person's word has the same or more value than a written agreement:
- in the logic of contract, decisions are written down in detail. Specific attention is given to formalisation.
- in the logic of consensus, the stakeholders are widely consulted. An extension of negotiations and the choice of "flexible" agreements, which sometimes conceal disagreements, are often observed.
- in the logic of honour, decisions are announced orally rather than r. in written form. There is much room for human relations, emotions and informal connections. Power-play is time-consuming.

▸ **Way in which power is shared**

Significant hierarchical distance versus *low hierarchical distance*: the level of hierarchical distance shows to which extent members having less power in the organisation accept this uneven distribution.

Observing the political, social and other institutions and determining their functioning methods can be a significant source of cultural learning.

Point 6 : Activity

Activity refers to the "physical demonstrations" connected to the action and work of a culture's members. In order to study it, we must first look into consumer patterns and "material" culture:

- *consumer patterns*: what people consume (the way they dress, what they eat, the way they move around..) are physical demonstrations of culture;
- *material culture*: the material culture refers to the physical and material symbols of a culture, such as a flag, a statue, etc.

Point 7 : Relation to uncertainty

The relation to uncertainty refers to the need of a society's individuals for certainty and predictability as well as to the way they apprehend risks.

High tolerance for uncertainty versus *low tolerance for uncertainty*: the level of tolerance for uncertainty indicates the extent to which individuals feel threatened by ambiguous and/or unexpected situations. It also indicates to which extent individuals have developed beliefs and institutions enabling them to avoid this kind of situations.

Point 8 : Reflection modes

The conceptual frameworks refer to a group's way of thinking. Analyzing conceptual frameworks means considering two points: the way a subject is considered and the way it is addressed.

▸ **The way a subject is considered**

Analytic approach versus *systemic approach*: in the analytic approach, more attention is given to the components than to the whole. Each issue or subject is dissected and analyzed part after part. On the other hand, in the systemic approach, more attention is paid to the whole than to the components. Each issue or subject is considered as a whole and emphasis is laid on the connections which might exist between the different components.

▸ **The way a subject is addressed**

Deductive approach versus *inductive approach*: in the deductive approach, emphasis is laid on theories and general principles. It is from these concepts and logical reasoning that practical applications and solutions will emerge. On the other hand, in the inductive approach, concrete situations and cases are the starting point of all reflections. General models and theories will be based upon intuitions.

Dialogue-oriented versus *data-oriented*: dialogue-oriented cultures consider interpersonal communication to be particularly important. In this kind of culture, it is essential to establish and maintain relations with others. It is necessary to go beyond the factual stage, which is only of relative importance. On the other hand, data-oriented cultures lay emphasis on the precision and importance of the information provided. Expectations stand rather at a factual level.

Point 9: Communication and relation patterns

Communication and relation patterns aim at defining the way individuals communicate as well as the relational mechanisms they trigger. To analyze communication and relation patterns, we need to look into three points: the way individuals express themselves, the way information circulates and the separation between private and public life.

▸ **The way individuals express themselves**

Verbal language predominance versus *non-verbal language predominance*: in terms of language, one form of language (verbal or non-verbal) has the upperhand in exchanges. The non-verbal language refers to gestures, movements, postures and appearances.

Direct approach versus *indirect approach*: in environments where direct approach prevails, individuals get straight to the point and favour the integrity of the message, risking offending or upsetting the other party. In the case of the indirect approach, the main objective will always be to maintain good relations. Divided opinions will tend not to be resolved, even if this could cause misunderstandings.

Formal approach versus *informal approach*: when the formal approach is applied, individuals rigorously respect protocols and rituals. In more informal approaches, people act in a more spontaneous and familiar way.

Neutrality versus *emotion*: in terms of reactions, do we expect from the members of an organisation to react in a rather neutral or emotional manner? In the so-called neutral cultures, the members of an organisation must control the expression of their feelings and their emotions in order to be objective. On the other hand, in the so-called emotional cultures, they must express their feelings as freely and openly as possible.

▶ **The way information circulates**

High context versus low context: the way information circulates in a society is highly dependant on its context. Implicit cultures are high context cultures. Information is not always transmitted through clear and explicit messages and must be deducted from the situation and the context itself. Information is usually easy to get and transmitted through the network. The language employed in the messages is usually quite informal. On the other hand, explicit cultures are low context cultures. Information is transmitted through clear, detailed and explicit messages and is segmented before the transmission. The speed of transmission is lower compared to implicit cultures. The language employed in the messages is usually specific and rather formal.

▶ **Separation between private and public life**

Specific approach versus generic approach: members of specific cultures usually consider it important to separate their professional life from the rest of their existence. Their public behaviour differs from their private behaviour. On the other hand, the members of generic cultures often consider that the integration of several aspects of their personality (family life, professional life, etc.) enables them to stabilise, develop and deepen their social relations. Their public and private behaviours are more alike.

Using the intercultural GPS to determine a profile

Experience is the better way to discover a culture. Differences between cultures appear by an effect of contrast. What appears to be reasonable and important in one culture may seem unreasonable or inadequate in another. Let us not forget that cultures are in constant evolution and that what is true nowadays may not be true in the future. Finally, differences may be observed even within a same culture and between social groups.

In this section, you will find two questionnaires which allowing to look into culture in a practical manner: one is oriented towards country culture and the other more specifically towards business culture. This list of questions is not exhaustive, but focuses on key points of the environment. We can only encourage you to contribute to this list and gradually customise it.

General questionnaire to decipher a culture

Questions regarding the relation to time
Variables to identify – *monochronic approach versus polychronic approach;* – *past-, present- or future- oriented;* – *monetary time versus factual time*
• Do people tend to do several things at the same time? • What is the importance given to the past, the present and the future respectively? • What does "be on time" mean? • How important is punctuality? • How important is the speed of execution?

Questions on rules, values and value orientation
Variables to identify – *masculinity versus femininity and any other value.*
• What are the features and attributes considered relevant or desirable or considered of little significance or undesirable? • Education: What are the purposes of education? Which are the favoured forms of learning? Which teaching and learning methods are used at home? What are the parents' expectations from their sons or daughters? • History and traditions: How are history and traditions transmitted to the next generations? How can cultural views of history be different from "scientific" facts or literal history? • Religion: What is the place of religion in society? Which religious roles and authorities are recognised? • The circle of life: What are the important stages, periods and transitions of life? Which behaviours are considered inappropriate or unacceptable for young children?

- Pets and animals: Which animals are highly valued and why? Which animals are considered appropriate or inappropriate to become pets?
- Expectations and aspirations: Do parents expect and hope that their children will integrate the prevailing culture, language or dialect? What are the expected cultural values preserved despite of the formal education level?
- Public holidays and celebrations: Which public holidays are celebrated? Why? Which holidays are important to children? Which cultural values are inculcated in children during their holidays?

Questions regarding the relation to the individual, actions and decisions

Variables to identify

– *pragmatic approach versus dogmatic approach;*
– *individualistic approach versus collectivist approach;*
– *"Do-er" attitude versus "be-er" attitude;*
– *Beliefs: of natural source versus of ideological source versus of relational source versus of factual source.*

- Who members of an organisation are they supposed to be looking after? Themselves and their close family – or the group they belong and "owe" their loyalty to?
- The family structure: Who is considered as member of the family? What rights, roles and responsibilities do the members have?
- What is the relation of man to nature? Is he supposed to adapt to it or to control it?
- How are phenomena, such as rain, lightings, flood, etc. explained?
- Are some behavioural taboos associated with natural phenomena?
- Is emphasis laid on the enforcement and respect of the rules or on the search for specific solutions?
- What kinds of arguments have the upper hand in discussions?
- Which factors may be regarded as source of truth?

Questions regarding the relation to space and territory

Variables to identify

– *private approach versus public approach;*
– *restricted informal space versus developed informal space;*
– *high space value versus moderate space value.*

- Which subjects are considered private and which are considered public? What do we have the "right" to talk about? Is family a topic to discuss?
- Which places are considered private and which are considered public? Is it common to invite colleagues at home or family members to corporate meetings?
- What is the desirable distance that we should keep between ourselves and our interlocutor? Between 15 and 45 cm? Between 45 and 75 cm? Between 75 cm and 1.25 metres?...
- Are there clear differences between offices?
- Is it important to have a vast or valuable space?

Questions regarding organisation

Variables to identify

– *Collaboration-oriented versus competition-oriented;*
– *universalist approach versus particularist approach;*
– *stability versus change;*
– *Prevailing managerial logic: contract versus consensus versus honour;*
– *significant hierarchical distance versus low hierarchical distance.*

- Political systems and institutions: How is political power shared? Which are the most influential political institutions? What is the importance of legislation?
- Social systems and organisations: How are people connected to each other? Which are the most influential social institutions?
- Economic system: What is the economic model in force? Liberal, partially liberal or communist?

- Work and spare time: Which occupations are considered as prestigious? Why? Is there a clear separation between professional and private life?
- How is power shared?
- To what extent does an organisation accept to unevenly share power?
- What are the roles available? For which persons? How are these roles acquired?
- How are ideas and opinions shared?
- Education: In the education of children, is emphasis laid on collaboration or on competition? The same question goes for other social systems.
- Do families and other institutions advocate change or stability?
- What is the role of rules? Is it only supportive or do rules have to be strictly applied, whatever the context?
- From what moment can we consider a deal as sealed?

Questions regarding activity

Variables to identify

– consumer patterns and material culture;
– describe the consumer pattern in its environment;
– what do people like by contrast and buy the most?
– how do they buy and consume products? Examples: the way people dress and their appearance, diet and food habits, way of life (spare time, working habits, etc.) and cultural material.

- Food: What do people eat, in what quantity and how many times? What are the good table manners?
- Clothing and personal appearance: How does the way people dress influence social identity? What is the concept and value of beauty and attractiveness?
- Art and music: Which forms of art and music are strongly valued? Which forms of art and music are considered appropriate for children?
- Identify strong cultural symbols like flags, hymns...

Questions regarding the relation to uncertainty

Variables to identify

– High tolerance for uncertainty versus low tolerance for uncertainty.

- What is the role of rules? Do people try to minimise risks through rules?

- Are rules numerous and complex, or limited to the strict minimum?
- How is risk-taking considered? Is it an established fact, a necessity or something to avoid?

Questions regarding reflection modes

Variables to identify

– analytical approach versus systemic approach;
– deductive approach versus inductive approach;
– Dialogue-oriented versus data-oriented.

- When there is a problem, is it considered from every angle or is a segmented approach adopted?
- In terms of approach, is emphasis laid on theories and general principles giving rise to practical applications and solutions. Or is emphasis laid on concrete facts considered as a starting point for reflection, giving rise to general standards and theories?
- What is more important in communication: data or dialogue?
- Health and hygiene: How are illnesses and death explained? How are specific illnesses treated?

Questions regarding communication and relation patterns

Variables to identify

– *verbal language predominance versus non-verbal language predominance;*
– *direct approach versus indirect approach;*
– *neutrality versus emotion;*
– *formal approach versus informal approach;*
– *high context versus low context; specific approach versus generic approach.*

- Which are the languages and dialects spoken?
- What is the importance of non verbal language compared to verbal language?
- In terms of approach and communication, are interlocutors expected to be direct and explicit, at the risk of offending or upsetting the other party? Or is a more indirect approach favoured, where the main objective is maintaining good relations?
- In terms of approach and communication, are interlocutors expected to react in a neutral or rather emotional manner? Is it better to control our emotions or to express them "freely"?
- How do people express their disagreement?
- How do people insult each other?
- How do they greet each other?
- How do they greet each other?
- Do individuals tend to strictly observe the protocols and rituals currently in force, or do they act in a more spontaneous and familiar way?
- What are the disciplinary means employed in order to ensure the respect of the protocol?
- How does information circulate? Rather orally or in written form?
- How do people use technology?
- How do people behave at home and in public?

Useful: provide details about environments
• Technological environment: what is the technological level ? How do people use technology? Do most people active in this environment have access to technology? • Economic environment: assess the economic situation of a country as well as the impact of globalisation. • Social environment: Assess the political situation of a country, the impact of globalisation and the social trend. • Political environment: assess the political situation of a country and the impact of globalisation.

Business questionnaire to decipher a culture

Provide details about customs observed in the business environment
• How are the first meetings carried-out? Is it necessary to be introduced by an acquaintance or is a direct contact sufficient? How do people introduce themselves? • Who are the people doing business, which methods do they use and why (what are their objectives)? • How do people get a good position in the business environment? • Which are the rules to be observed? • Is it recommended to invest time in establishing relations and building trust beforehand? Or is it enough to establish contact with the interlocutor when an opportunity for a deal arises? • Where, how and when should a meeting be organised? • Negotiation process: How to start a negotiation? How to take a stand? Who negotiates? How fast is the negotiation process? How to close a negotiation? • How are agreements implemented? • etc.

Elements to be taken into consideration when using the intercultural GPS in the framework of negotiations

Avoid the oversimplified binary approach

Any cultural dimension is potentially "good" or "bad", beneficial or harmful. In order to be able to capitalise on cultural differences, it is essential to understand the content of each dimension. Wealth comes with understanding.

A binary approach of cultural dimensions leads individuals to choose one cultural orientation rather than another. This simplified approach prevents the consideration of new perspectives and the reconciliation of the different alternatives. This way of thinking is selective to the extent that if one option is considered to be "true", the other one is considered to be "false" by contrast.

It is rather recommended to look into contrasts and oppositions. That is because new ideas and thoughts emerge from confrontation. This way of thinking is also called dialectics.

Avoid confusion between culture, ideology and personality

Anything the group thinks, says and does belongs to culture. Each individual is surrounded by his/her own culture, which is an integral part of him/her. Culture influences the way we live, perceive our environment and die. Culture is therefore omnipresent and influential. From that point, one may easily conclude that "everything is cultural". Yet, culture cannot account for everything. It is essential to also take into account the prevailing ideology and the personalities of our negotiating partners. The experiences of each individual have a bearing on their line of action and the way they contemplate their own existence.

Assessing culture

The form opposite may prove helpful to characterize a culture. Evaluate each dimension using the following ascending scales, from 0 to 5.

In addition to the analysis provided below, we recommend to take notes

Table 2.1

Dimension	Category											Dimension
	Assessment											
	5	4	3	2	1	0	1	2	3	4	5	
1. Relation to time												
Monochronism	5	4	3	2	1	0	1	2	3	4	5	Polychronism
Past-oriented	5	4	3	2	1	0	1	2	3	4	5	Present-oriented
Future-oriented	5	4	3	2	1	0						
Monetary time	5	4	3	2	1	0	1	2	3	4	5	Factual time
2. Rules, values and value orientation												
Masculinity	5	4	3	2	1	0	1	2	3	4	5	Feminity
Other	5	4	3	2	1	0	1	2	3	4	5	Other
3. Relation to the individual, actions and decisions												
Pragmatic approach	5	4	3	2	1	0	1	2	3	4	5	Dogmatic approach
"Do-er" attitude	5	4	3	2	1	0	1	2	3	4	5	"Be-er" attitude
Individualistic approach	5	4	3	2	1	0	1	2	3	4	5	Collectivistic approach
Beliefs originating from facts	5	4	3	2	1	0	1	2	3	4	5	Beliefs originating from nature
Beliefs originating from relations	5	4	3	2	1	0	1	2	3	4	5	Beliefs originating from ideology
4. Relation to space and territory												
Developed informal space	5	4	3	2	1	0	1	2	3	4	5	Restricted informal space
High space value	5	4	3	2	1	0	1	2	3	4	5	Moderate space value
Private approach	5	4	3	2	1	0	1	2	3	4	5	Public approach

Dimension	Category Assessment	Dimension
	5. Organisation	
	Political, social, legal institutions…	
Competition-oriented	5 4 3 2 1 0 1 2 3 4 5	Collaboration-oriented
Universalist approach	5 4 3 2 1 0 1 2 3 4 5	Particularist approach
Stability	5 4 3 2 1 0 1 2 3 4 5	Change
Managerial logic: contract	5 4 3 2 1 0 1 2 3 4 5	Managerial logic: consensus
Managerial logic: logic: honour	5 4 3 2 1 0	
High hierarchical distance	5 4 3 2 1 0 1 2 3 4 5	Low hierarchical distance
	6. Activity	
Consumer patterns	Write your observations here	
Material Culture	Write your observations here	
	7. Relation to uncertainty	
High tolerance for uncertainty	5 4 3 2 1 0 1 2 3 4 5	Low tolerance for uncertainty
	8. Reflection modes	
Analytical approach	5 4 3 2 1 0 1 2 3 4 5	Systemic approach
Deductive approach	5 4 3 2 1 0 1 2 3 4 5	Inductive approach
Data-oriented	5 4 3 2 1 0 1 2 3 4 5	Dialogue-oriented

Dimension	Category											Dimension
	Assessment											
9. Communication and relation patterns												
Verbal language predominance	5	4	3	2	1	0	1	2	3	4	5	Non-verbal language predominance
Direct approach	5	4	3	2	1	0	1	2	3	4	5	Indirect approach
Formal approach	5	4	3	2	1	0	1	2	3	4	5	Informal approach
Neutrality	5	4	3	2	1	0	1	2	3	4	5	Emotion

Conclusion

Culture is comprehensive and omnipresent. The intercultural GPS enables individuals to understand complex realities in a simple manner. In this book, it is applied to the field of negotiation and giving the reader the possibility to actively capitalise on cultural differences by turning them into assets. Like other tools, the intercultural GPS must be used with caution. It is important to remember that there are no true or false approaches, but only specific answers to given issues.

PART 2

INTERCULTURAL NEGOTIATION METHOD

"Systematic innovation requires a willingness to look on change as an opportunity."
Peter Drucker

There are several methods of international negotiation. In this book, we present the SNA method (Successful Negotiation Activator), which allows users to approach all types of negotiation peacefully and efficiently. By integrating the intercultural GPS into the process, we underline the international aspect of human relations.

The SNA method in brief

"Successful Negotiation Activator" (by Manoëlla Wilbaut)		
Fundamentals of negotiation		
Make sure the **balance of power** is favourable to you Manage the negotiation **climate** Manage the negotiation **stages** Make sure you remain in the negotiation **zone** Adapt your **language** Use the power of **listening** and **asking questions**		
How to prepare negotiation?	**How to conduct negotiation?**	**How to conclude the negotiation and consider future prospects?**
First contact: find out how to get in touch with the other party	**Start:** start the negotiation	*Conclude the negotiation by yourself*
Parties: identify the negotiating parties	**Real requests:** clarify the real requests of the other party	**Key problems:** make sure major problems are resolved
Objectives, negotiation threshold and common ground: identify the negotiators' objectives, determine the negotiation threshold and find common ground		
Motivations and influences: find out what influences and motivates parties	**Dynamics:** manage group dynamics	**Conclusion:** introduce the conclusion
	Proposals: make proposals	
Situation analysis: analyze the situation (i.e. compare objectives to available resources and constraints)	**Activation:** make progress in the negotiation	**Last offer:** make a last offer and go beyond the possible reluctance of the other party
Negotiating style & strategy: chose a negotiating style, identify the other party's style and elaborate a negotiation strategy	**Reactions:** respond to the other party's proposals and reactions	
Organisation: organise the meeting and interactions a) Identify practices in terms of protocol and communication b) Identify entertainment habits c) Use the venue and agenda of the negotiation as a tool		**Conclude the negotiation with the support of one or several third parties**
	Stand: take a stand	**Application:** apply decisions taken
		Future: consider future prospects

Figure II.1 – The SNA tool (M. Wilbaut)

Culture has a bearing on negotiation, the parties to it and the way they interact. These combined elements determine the final result of a negotiation. In the field of international negotiations, it is essential to draw a distinction between the following elements:
- culture;
- negotiating parties (people);
- situation (framework);
- negotiation process (interactions);
- result.

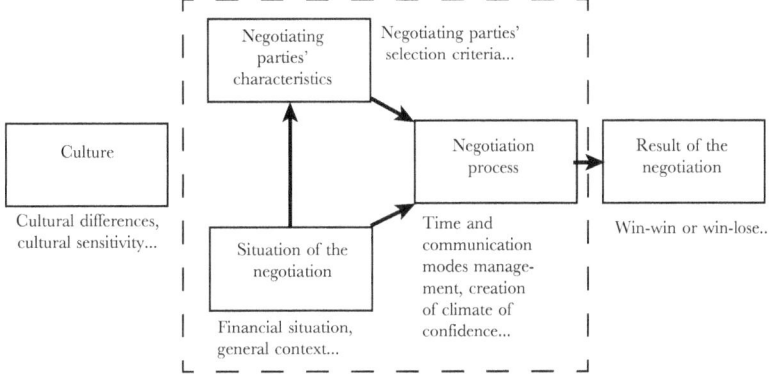

Figure II.2 – Intercultural approach of negotiation

In international negotiations, even more than in local negotiations, the difference between the process and the content of the negotiation must be clear. The process relates to interpersonal interactions and the way things go on, while the content refers to the "raw material" of negotiation. In a computer context, for instance, the content would refer to the *hardware*, while the process would refer to the *software*.

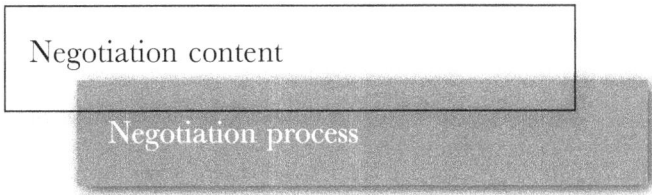

Figure II.3 – Distinction between the content and the process (or form) of negotiation

The SNA method seen from an intercultural perspective

In order to combine the SNA method and the intercultural GPS, two phases are necessary:
- identifying the fundamental variables of negotiation;
- identifying the impact of culture on these variables.

Identifying the fundamental variables of negotiation

The social and cultural environment influences the way people negotiate. Identifying the variables of a negotiation allows you to assess the extent to which the environment has a bearing on the negotiation process. We identified thirteen fundamental variables:

1. Choice of negotiators: what are the best criteria for choosing negotiators? Status? Expertise? Personal attributes?
2. Situation analysis: which are the methods used to analyze the situation? How does information circulate in the system?
3. Bases and priorities of negotiation: how do negotiators perceive the negotiation? Is the negotiation competition oriented or problem-solving oriented? What are the objectives and priorities of the negotiation? What is the role of entertainment during the negotiation process?
4. Choice of a strategy and style of negotiation: shall we choose a rather collaborative or competitive style? Which is the best strategy for remaining in the negotiation zone? Are risky strategies promoted?
5. First contact and organisation of the meeting: what are the conventions to observe at first contact? What are the best conditions of the first meeting? Is it better to choose a discreet or an extravagant venue? Should the agenda be tight or rather flexible?
6. Beginning of the negotiation: How does the negotiation start? Is it important to respect the protocol?
7. Communication: information, proposals, counter-proposals and positions: What kinds of issues are put forward? How and when are proposals made? How do the parties take a stand?
8. Decision making and implementation of the agreement: How are decisions taken and by whom? What makes the decision official?
9. Results and future prospects: What are the expected results? Rather short-term or long-term results? How do parties consider future relations?

10. Rhythm and evolution of the negotiation: How are the negotiation stages managed? How much time is dedicated to the different stages? What is the rhythm of the negotiation and who gets to chose this rhythm?
11. Persuasion and progress of the negotiation: How do parties try to influence one another and what are the underlying channels enabling them to achieve expected results?
12. Power balance and climate management: How to manage variables relating to the negotiation climate (time, space and mood) to achieve the expected result? How does power balance tend to be established? Which are the favoured or forbidden techniques?
13. Notion of trust: what is the way to earn the other parties' trust?

Table II.1 – Table combining the negotiation variables with the SNA as it was presented.

Throughout the negotiation process		
Rhythm and evolution of the negotiation		
Persuasion & progress of the negotiation		
Power balance and climate management		
Notion of trust		
Step 1: Prepare negotiation	**How to conduct negotiation?**	**How to conclude the negotiation and consider future prospects?**
Choice of negotiators	Beginning of the negotiation	Decision making and implementation of the agreement
Situation analysis	Communication: information, proposals, counter-proposals and positions	**Results and future prospects**
Bases and priorities of negotiation		
Choice of a strategy and style of negotiation		
First contact and organisation of the meeting		

Identifying the impact of culture on these variables

Table II.2° – Impact of culture on negotiation – Summary (M. Wilbaut)

	Relation to time	Norms, tablevalues and value orientation	Relation to the individual, actions and decisions	Relation to space and territory	Organisation	Activity	Relation to uncertainty	Reflection mode	Communication and relation patterns
Choice of negotiators	X	X	X	X	X	X	X	X	X
Situation analysis			X						X
Bases and priorities of negotiation		X					X		
Choice of a strategy and style of negotiation	X	X	X		X		X	X	
First contact and organisation of the meeting	X	X	X		X	X			X
Beginning of the negotiation	X			X					X
Communication: information, proposals, counter-proposals and positions	X	X	X		X		X	X	X
Decision making and implementation of the agreement	X		X		X		X		X
Results and future prospects	X	X			X				
Rhythm and evolution of the negotiation	X		X		X		X	X	
Persuasion & way of getting negotiation further	X	X	X		X		X	X	
Power balance and climate management	X	X		X	X	X			
Notion of trust	X	X	X		X	X		X	X

The columns present the cultural dimensions, while the rows present the fundamental variables of negotiation. The symbol X indicates by which cultural dimensions the negotiation variables are the most influenced. In order to illustrate these different points, many examples will be presented in the following chapters.

In order to achieve quality, it is necessary to have efficient tools and to be flexible so as to use them in an integrated and relevant manner. At this stage, it is important to have an overview of the situation and to identify the key elements and turning points of the negotiation process. This is even more the case in international negotiations.

The thirteen fundamental variables of negotiation vary from one culture to another. Keeping this list in mind allows negotiators to judge more precisely the exact way culture influences on the negotiation process.

CHAPTER 3

THE KEYS TO A SUCCESSFUL INTERCULTURAL NEGOTIATION

"Being tactful in audacity is knowing how far one can go too far."
Jean Cocteau

Subject: Know the "golden" rules to be respected throughout the negotiation.

The SNA negotiation tool puts forward six core principles to be respected throughout the negotiation:

- make sure the balance of power is favourable to you;
- manage the negotiation climate;
- manage the negotiation stages;
- remain in the negotiation zone;
- adapt your language;
- use the power of listening and asking questions.

These principles are more linked with the negotiation process (or the way it develops) than to the subject treated, i.e. the container rather than the contents. The results of many negotiations are disappointing, because negotiators have neglected some elements of the negotiation process.

Make sure the balance of power is favourable to you

The notion of power is subjective. It is necessary to distinguish its content (or the real relative power of each party) from the process (or the relative perception of each party's power).

The most important thing in negotiation is not the real power you have, but rather the power your interlocutor thinks you have. Therefore, before starting a negotiation, it is highly recommended to strengthen the perception of your position of your interlocutor as well as people around him.

The levers of power and how to use them

In order to act on the balance of power, it is important to have trump cards up your sleeve. These are part of the raw materials of negotiation. They can include "sanctions", potential "concessions" or constructive proposals. There is a distinction between having a trump and being willing to use it. One of the difficulties arising during negotiations is to estimate the extent to which the other party is willing to make use of his trump cards.

The use of some "cards" is more restrictive than others. Therefore, it is necessary to take stock of the situation and assess as fairly as possible the challenges, cost and real impact of using a trump card, for oneself as well as for the other party.

The negotiators' "cards" can be put together in nine levers[9] or "power cursors" (figure 3.1).

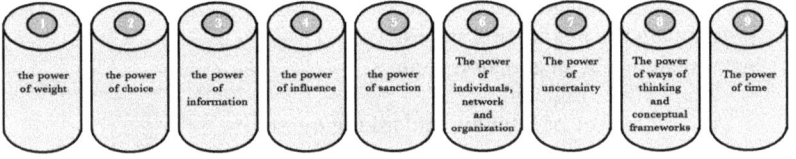

Figure 3.1 – Nine Levers of power

1. *The power of weight* refers to the importance one negotiator attaches to another.
2. *The power of choice* is the ability of one of the negotiators to find other offers and partners. Is the situation characterised as monopolistic or oligopolistic?
3. *The power of information* refers to the ability of one party to obtain information about the other party (concerning offers, resources, constraints, etc.).
4. *The power of influence* is the ability of one of the parties to influence, directly or indirectly, the interests of the other party. The power of influence may take various forms. Here are some examples:

---

9   Adaptation and improvement of Philippe Korda's list of power cursors comprising 6 elements: the power of weight, the power of choice, the power of information, the power of influence, the power of time and the power of sanction. P. Korda, *Négocier et défendre ses marges*, 4th edition, Dunod, 2010.

a) the power of values refers to the ability of one of the parties to understand and use the values of the other party in order to get closer to it;
b) the power of communication and relation patterns refers to the ability of one party to adapt to the languages and relevant communication methods and use them in order to influence the other party;
c) the power of space refers to the ability of one party to use the space as a source of competitive advantage;
d) the power of habits and customs refers to the ability of one of the parties to understand and use the habits and customs of the other party in order to get closer to it.

5. *The power of sanction* refers to the ability of one of the parties to harm or, alternatively, to reward the other party.
6. *The power of the individuals, network and organisation* refers to the ability of one party to act and use the network and surrounding organisational structures to have an impact on the other party.
7. *The power of uncertainty* refers to the parties' need for security and their tendency to take risks.
8. *The power of the ways of thinking and conceptual frameworks* refers to the ability of one party to assimilate the operation method of the other party and to use this knowledge to get closer to it.
9. *The power of time* refers to the competitive advantage or alternatively the constraints that time may represent for the negotiating parties.

Generally speaking, no one has all the trump cards and no one is totally deprived of them. We must identify the real trump cards we possess as well as those the other party could reasonably think we do. There are two ways to influence the balance of power:
- neutralising the effect of the other party's strategies: identifying the tactics used by the other party usually allows you to reduce or even eliminate their impact;
- having a real effect on the balance of power: to this end, negotiators deliberately use competitive or cooperative strategies.

List of key tactics enabling to influence the balance of power

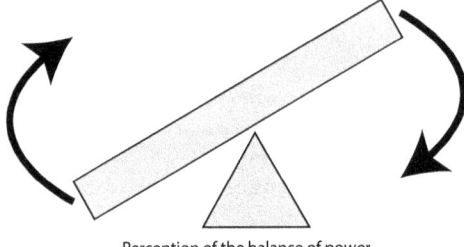

Perception of the balance of power

Figure 3.2 – Perception of the balance of powers

You will find below a list of tactics classified according to their use:
- *Conversation leading/structuring tactics* are used in order to give structure to the negotiation. They define the framework of exchanges. Therefore, to put them into practice, it is better to have already thought about the possible evolution of the conversation.
- The *argument tactics* can be used during discussions without specific preparation. These tactics are rhetorical tools, techniques to be used in order to emphasise an argument or to cope with an unexpected situation.

The tactics mentioned below are of a "positive nature". Other tactics, of negative nature, are mentioned separately, as they are rarely beneficial in the long term.

▸ Conversation leading /structuring tactics

In this category we find:
- step-by-step tactics, aiming at banking on progressive aspects of a negotiation;
- role-playing tactics, using the setting of the scene as a source of competitive advantage;
- perception-influencing tactics, banking on appearance rather than reality;
- tactics concerning the use of limits and resources, using assets and objectives as negotiation components;
- push tactics, usually resorting to force and exaggeration;
- suggestion tactics, based more on what we let people think than on what we say;
- indirect tactics, where apparent objectives differ from the actual ones.

3. The keys to a successful intercultural negotiation

Step-by-step strategies

Progressive method: this method aims at obtaining compensation or at having the other party accept an offer by progressively presenting it.

Presenting an offer in two steps: This tactic lays on the fact that, according to several studies, an offer is more likely to be accepted if presented in two steps rather than one. This fact was highlighted in 1986 by American psychologist J. Burger who called this tactic the "That's-not-all technique". Let us consider the following situation[10]: at a local fair, different cakes are presented on a stand. When buyers ask for the price of a cake, they are offered a cake and two biscuits for 75 cents (€). Some others are told by the salesperson that a piece of cake costs 75 cents. Then, after a brief discussion with his colleague, the salesperson explains that for the same price they also get two biscuits for free. We observed that in 72% of the clients buy the cake and biscuits, while only 44% do so in the first case.

Use of margins: make two or more requests that get you closer to the final objective in order to reduce the margin of error.

Role-playing strategies

Call in an accomplice: use another person in order to gain the trust of the other party.

Play the good and the bad guy: this tactic often implies the presence of two persons who adopt opposite behaviours. One is being aggressive while the other is much more accommodating and may even go as far as to regret his colleague's behaviour.

Jeckill and Hyde: This is a variation on the good and bad guy's tactic. It consists in being alternately aggressive and curt and then open and accommodating towards the other party.

Play the role of the agent with limited authority: act as if you were in the service of a superior who gives instructions and is responsible for the final approval.

Play the fake decision-maker: this tactic consists in leading a negotiation as if you were the decision-maker. Once you have obtained as much advantages as expected, you go back to square one on the pretext that you need the approval of a superior, of another department...

---

10 Nicolas Gueguen, *Cent petites expériences en psychologie du consommateur*, Paris, Dunod, 2005.

Do not give away all your cards at once: this tactic consists in keeping cards up your sleeve and only use them gradually.

Hide your objective: this tactic aims at hiding your true objective from the other party (by avoiding to make specific requests or even by not making any request at all in connection with your real needs) and to wear him/her out on a point of secondary importance in order to discover the other party's actual objective.

Perception-influencing tactics

Combine or divide the requests: combine several requests into one or, alternatively, divide one request into several parts.

Reduce the value of an offer: consists in minimising the other party's offer by putting things into perspective and in some cases by comparing it to the competitor's offer.

Bidding and invitation to tender: consists in getting the other party to react against a third party, whether it exists or not.

Play with levels: change, in different ways, the level of implication. For example, switch from a personal level to an organisational, national or international level.

Divide up differences: this enables you to reduce their perceived importance. This tactic is useful to quickly bridge the gap between the parties.

Tactics concerning the use of limits and resources

The precondition: consists in setting out a condition related to the opening of negotiations.

Play with time: speed up or slow down time; arrive in advance or late…

Present an ultimatum: make a clear "take it or leave it" offer. You must make sure the offer is credible and that you are not being offensive.

Set limits: in order to set the framework for the evolution of the negotiation. Different types of limits can be set: geographical, financial, availability limits, etc. The following tactic is a special limit-setting case.

Set a deadline: many concessions are the result of time pressure.

Push tactics

Over-dramatisation: the idea is to paint a black picture of the situation, to show your concerns and pass them on to the other party so as to eventually present your offer as the solution to this shared problem.

Pull all the stops out: this tactic aims at favourably influencing the other party by presenting carefully your offer amongst others.

Introduce fake requests: introduce "imaginary" problems in order to conceal your real interests. This tactic gives more room for manoeuvre when dealing with concessions at a later stage. The three following tactics fall under the same category.

Make several consecutive requests: put pressure on the other party and force him/her to accept one of your requests; probably the less inconvenient to him/her.

Put pressure: consists in unsettling the other party by different means.

Swamp the other party with information: go into many unnecessary details covering a broad spectrum.

Make a concrete concession in exchange of a future commitment: known as the "carrot and stick", this tactic consists in getting an immediate advantage by letting the other party hope he will get something in the future.

Suggestion tactics

Make a hypothetical suggestion: in order to put the other party to the test. Example "what... if...".

Ask for participation: of the other party in order to solve a problem; encourage the other party to explain what s/he would do in your situation.

Indirect tactics

Use paradoxical intention: get the other party to do something while pretending you do not wish him/her to.

Switch the negotiator(s): unsettle the other party by introducing one or several new negotiators. This strategy is unsettling because the relation needs to be rebuilt and/or the background is usually unknown.

▶ **Argument tactics**

Role-playing tactics

Play bulldog: be relatively unpleasant with the other party in order to give as few information as possible about your interests and maybe also to undermine the other party's position.

Be cold and silent: do not be talkative and give away no emotions. The goals are the same with the bulldog tactic but the form is different, more respectful.

Call upon a "fake friend" or an authority: lead the other party to think that you are not free to act as you please and that a third party will influence the decision, whether be it a superior, a colleague...

Call upon a third party: involve other people, such as renowned experts, or suggest taking their opinions into account.

Seem naïve and curious: play fool and ask questions. Once you get the answer, pretend to be leaving and then come back with a detail which "destroys" the explanation you were given.

Feign ignorance: pretend you do not understand or cannot manage to remember.

Bluff: make the other party believe you have more information or advantages. It is an overbid in comparison with reality.

Reverse the roles: suggest that the two parties exchange their roles for a predefined period of time.

Make reference to an authority: legal, corporate or any authority supporting your opinion.

Perception-influencing tactics

Enhance the value of granted advantages: the point is to present the concessions put forward as tangible solutions, so that the other party realises their value.

Putting emphasis on free will: underlining their freedom makes people more favourably disposed to do what we ask from them.

Tactics concerning the use of limits and resources

Turn over the other party's strength: consists in using the other party's position, principles or assertions to strengthen your own position.

Go beyond claims and other such points: keep going beyond the other party's claims by presenting better examples.

Put forward the budget limit: show your real interest while confessing a personal budget limit. This technique is very efficient as it is not based on the appreciation of a product or of its price. Nevertheless, the efficiency of this method is based on the credibility of your claim.

Come back to previously resolved problems: this tactic consists in backtracking.

Ask for a postponement or delay the answer: this gives you time to think or to obtain more information or equipment.

Push tactics

Challenge: challenge the other party to do something in order to get him to agree with you.

Use baits or lures: consists in revealing pieces of information "by mistake" in order to motivate the other party as well as to encourage and facilitate concessions.

Stick to your line: consists in not giving ground, respectfully and firmly. This tactic can be used for a specific, non negotiable point.

Destabilisation: aims at leaving the other party completely at loss (by means of humour, aggressive behaviour, traveling...) either to counter a difficult argument or to create artificial tensions.

Arouse emotions: in a negotiation, arousing another party's emotions may be a good thing, whether these emotions are positive (like complicity or friendship) or even negative (like anger or despondency). To achieve this goal, we recommend using evocative and concrete words which bring images to the mind.

Create surprise by bringing about radical change or by acting the opposite way of what is expected: bring about unexpected change.

Suggestion tactics

Admit to mistakes: if in a predicament, admit your mistake, apologise and accept the reprimand if it is proportional.

Take stock of the situation: summarise briefly and regularly the situation, emphasising the common ground and points of agreement identified so far.

Claim it is a special case: underline the specificity of the problem and say it deserves specific attention or even a special treatment.

Appeal to reciprocity: make concessions (often of minor importance to start with) and ask the other party to return the favour.

Surrender or give in: when in weak position, withdraw and ask the other party to make allowances.

Indirect tactics

Maieutics: consists in asking a series of questions leading to positive or "obvious" answers. Questions follow on in a way that enables you to get the other party exactly where you want.

Withdraw: refuse to go on with the negotiation. If you are just bluffing, it is important to provide yourself with a way back. The following strategy is similar to this one.

Change of environment: modify the other party's comfort zone.

Take note without debate: it is a typical tactic enabling you to refute the other party's criticism or attacks without starting a controversy. It consists in showing your understanding or empathy for the other party, or simply in taking note of his remarks without starting a debate on the points s/he is trying to raise.

Transfer: consists in transferring a request of the other party from a deadlock to a concession you are willing to make.

The following tactics are of a negative nature and are usually not recommended. Nevertheless, it is important to be able to identify and inhibit them:

- discredit some associations: associate the other party, entirely or partially, to dubious or offensive connections. The following strategy is rather similar to this one.
- make negative comments: put the other party on the defensive by making negative comments (for example by questioning his/her position, approach…).
- use biased examples: deliberately use only limited information, such as statistics, or some pieces of information to illustrate one's point.
- misinterpret deliberately: deliberately misinterpret the other party's behaviours and act accordingly.

- simulate a disagreement between negotiators on the same side: ideally between the "good" and the "bad" guy. This leads the other party to agree with the most reasonable approach.
- deceive the other party: make an unrealistic offer and deceive the other party by finding at the last moment a reason to change your mind.
- present the other party with a fait accompli: act unilaterally and, observe the other party's reaction from that position.
- show your anger, be it feigned or real: this is an emotional intimidation strategy. Showing one's anger helps to underline the importance of the situation. The following strategy is similar to this one.
- be irrational: act in an irrational or at least unusual manner to unsettle the other party.
- act aggressively: this tactic sometimes allows you to obtain very short-term results, but it rather usually prompts the other party to backtrack and withdraw from the negotiation.
- threaten: express your will to prejudice the other party's interests and warn him/her of the consequences.

Case studies

Use of time in your tactics in order to favourably influence the situation

CH   RU   UA

In China, like in Russia and Ukraine, patience is considered a virtue. In contrast, executives coming from western countries have the reputation of being impatient. It is possible that the Chinese, Russians and Ukrainians use time in their negotiation tactics by bringing negotiations beyond the deadlines in order to gain an advantage or even by trying to re-negotiate the agreement at the end of the process, even after the contract has been signed. Time is a significant power lever in negotiation.

Strategies to be avoided in Spain and in Mexico

ES MX

In terms of behaviour, the Mexicans lay emphasis on a person's dignity, whatever his/her social status or personal wealth. The same goes for Spain, where the principles according to which all men are equal and each individual is unique are fundamental.

Therefore, it is important to spend time getting to know everyone and, above all, it is essential to never adopt any behaviour that could humiliate somebody in public. So, some negotiation tactics are to be avoided for obvious reasons.

Strategies to use in case of mistake or negligence

JP

In case of mistake or negligence, apologising may prove to be a good strategy in Japan. In these cases, individuals (as well as companies) are expected to apologise. In the case of a company, the apology must come from the highest levels of hierarchy. Apologising shows that you are respectful and that you understand your mistake. The same does not apply for companies where the notion of assertiveness is much stronger and where such a line of conduct would probably be taken as a mark of weakness.

Using common sense and pragmatism as power lever

BE

Belgian people are very pragmatic. Given the diversity of the Belgian population, the search for compromises and creative solutions has become an integral part of the national culture. Showing common sense is an important power lever in negotiations with Belgians.

Managing the negotiation climate

The psychological climate of a negotiation is the pervading general atmosphere. The climate influences the negotiation process and impacts on the final result. For this reason, seasoned negotiators use climate as a real negotiation tool. Managing the climate of a negotiation means managing the three following variables: time, space and mood. Note that two other variables or elements could also be taken into consideration: trust and self-esteem. The climate created before, during and after the negotiation must always be in line with the adopted strategy and the expected results (figure 3.3).

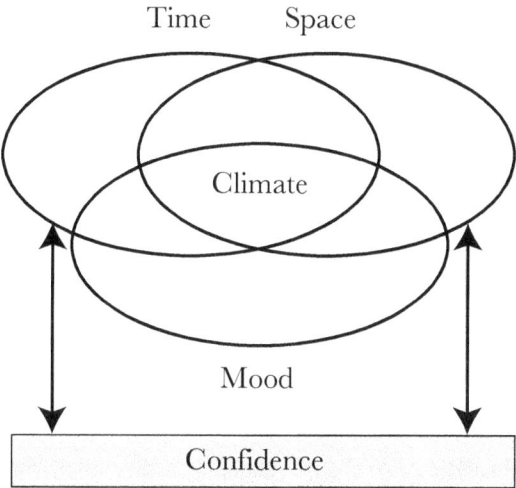

Figure 3.3 – The components of climate

Time

In negotiation, whatever the subject considered (beginning the negotiation, introducing problematic issues, making concessions, etc), it is recommended to chose the right time in order to bring it forward.

In terms of time management, table 3.1 provides some examples of competitive and cooperative signals.

Table 3.1 Examples of time signals

Competitive signals	Cooperative signals
• Starting the meeting early in the morning • Having a strict and tight agenda • Not planning breaks • ...	• Starting the meeting later • Have a flexible agenda • Planning some breaks • ...

Table 3.2 Critical points related to time in the framework of negotiations

1. Prepare the negotiation and take advantage of the time before the negotiation
• Take the time to prepare for the negotiation, build relations between the parties, lobby and eventually to develop strategic alliances. • If you do not have much time, clearly identify the incomplete preparation stages. • Whatever the amount of time you have, the following question must never be eluded: "what are the other party's needs?"

2. Assess the rhythm and total duration of the negotiation
• Determine the best time to start the negotiation (hour/day/month/year) by taking into account the preferences and cultural differences of every party. • Use strategies to give rhythm to the negotiation, for example: – to slow down the process, postpone meetings frequently or make long speeches; – to speed up the process, clearly specify the time limits. 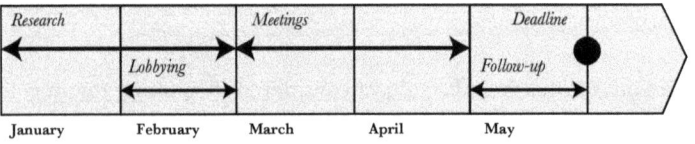

3. Possibility of setting time limits
Unless you have a good reason, it is preferable not to present the other party with an ultimatum. Approaching the end of an deadline increases pressure.

4. Choose the moment to conclude
Carefully choose the right moment to make your final offer and conclude the negotiation.

5. Take advantage of the time following the negotiation
A negotiation is concluded only when all parties reach an agreement and formally seal their agreement by determining which actions must be taken by whom and when. The follow-up of the agreement must also be planned.

Space

The venue of the negotiation must be carefully chosen. In absolute terms, there are no good or bad venues. It is only a question of perception. No change of venue must be suggested before evaluating the impact on the negotiation. In the case that a negotiation is supposed to take place in several sessions, the parties can decide to alternate venues.

Table 3.3. Advantages of a venue as opposed to another

Advantages of using the other party's venue	Advantages of using your venue
Demonstration of the other party's importance or demonstration of respect.	Psychological advantage if the other party comes to your meeting place.
Possible access to a superior authority.	Enhancing the feeling of dominance or assertiveness.
Saving time as you do not have to prepare the venue (and possibility to ask for changes in case something is not suitable).	Possibility to lay out the physical environment in such a way, so as to influence the negotiation climate.

Advantages of using the other party's venue	Advantages of using your venue
Possibility to withdraw more easily (it is easier to leave the other party's office than yours).	Better control over the negotiation rhythm (planning of interruptions, extension or early closing of the negotiation).
Withholding of information if needed (it is easier to say you did not bring the information with you).	Obtaining quickly the necessary information.
Postponement of the final decision if needed (for example on the pretext of having to finalise your report first).	Obtaining quickly the approval needed.
Possibility to get a draft report underlining the other party's commitments.	Opportunity to draw up the agreement immediately.
Opportunity to use the other party's facilities which you may not have.	Strong atmosphere of trust as you know the ground.

▶ **Space factors used to influence climate**

These are the six following points:

- atmosphere: venue, furnishings, decoration, lighting;
- furniture and environment: table, office, chairs;
- seats arrangement: possibility of visual contacts and expected interpersonal distances;
- equipment: communication equipment, visual aid;
- personal comfort: drinks, toilets;
- personal presentation – choice of clothes, accessories.

Negotiations can take place anywhere. There is no predefined venue. Negotiations can be carried out in an office, a meeting room, a restaurant… or even in a place without any meeting rooms. When the time comes to choose a venue, some practical points must be considered: number of participants, easy access to the meeting rooms, cultural norms required for the participants, etc. In male dominated cultures, such as those in Arab countries, it is recommended to meet in "impressive" places.

Once the venue is defined, decorative elements can be added to influence the environment. The use of academic books, professional reviews or technical drawings creates an impressive environment while the use of flowers or even of non technical reviews creates a more informal environment. The colour of a room is also significant. Warm colours like green, yellow or orange create a more collaborative atmosphere than dark colours.

It is important to make sure participants are comfortable by controlling factors, such as the room temperature, proper functioning of the ventilation and lighting system. The choice of furniture is also very important. The size and shape of tables should also be taken into account. Rectangular tables are more formal and strict while round tables are more informal. Other options can also be considered: T- or U- shaped tables, etc. The type of chairs can also send a signal to the other party. Are the seats large and comfortable or are they purely functional? Note that in some cases, the negotiating parties will deliberately supply an insufficient number of chairs in order to have some people standing. Three elements must be considered when arranging furniture in a room, particularly tables and chairs: visual contact, proximity and personal space. Decide if you wish to have visual contact with the other party or not. People sitting side by side usually find visual contacts less conflictive than when sitting face to face. The distance between people also has an impact on negotiation. The greater the distance, the more formal the meeting will be. On the other hand, people sitting too close to each other tend to feel uncomfortable. And of course, we should not forget cool drinks.

Finally, your presentation as well as the presentation of your team members must go in line with the message you wish to convey. Be aware of the impact of your appearance – clothes, accessories, hairstyle, etc. – on the other party.

Mood

A negotiator's behaviour is the result of his/her mood.

▶ Mood factors used to influence the negotiation climate

These are the four following points:
- language used – the choice of words and sentences;
- tone and rhythm of the voice;
- language structure – the amount of questions compared to the amount of assertions;
- capacity to listen.

▶ Assessment of negotiators' mood

The negotiators' mood can be assessed according to a certain amount of dimensions.

Table 3.4 – Example of dimensions used to assess the other party's mood

Informal	*versus*	Formal
Easy-going	*versus*	Tense
Confident	*versus*	Suspicious
Collaborative	*versus*	Defensive
Friendly	*versus*	Hostile
Reasonable	*versus*	Irrational
Useful (helpful)	*versus*	Cumbersome
Creative, fluent	*versus*	Rigid, Steady

▶ **Interaction of time, space and mood variables**

Consciously managing these three factors enables you to manage climate and, consequently, to strongly influence the development and result of the negotiation.

Importance of trust and self-esteem

Trust and self-esteem are two additional elements to be taken into account. Evolving in a climate of trust in which all parties are comfortable is important to be successful in a negotiation.

▶ **Convert trust into predictability**

The lack of trust of the other party is the main reason of failure of the negotiations. Parties who do not trust one another are less keen to cooperate and find an agreement satisfying both of them. If you do not trust the other party, it is unwise to discuss this point with him/her, as this could create a very negative emotional climate. Once personally offended, the other party may stick to his/her guns and, in return, question your reliability. Rather than questioning the other party's reliability, it would be better to look for solutions in order to guarantee an acceptable level of predictability. To achieve this, you must concentrate on mechanisms allowing you to assess if, or even guarantee that the other party will stick to his/her commitments. We talk of predictability when the other party acts in the expected way. Evolving in a more predictable climate can lead to a more trusting negotiation atmosphere.

▶ **Self-esteem**

Most people prefer getting positive messages. Acknowledging the other party's need for respect can positively influence the negotiation climate. Attacking the other party on a personal level leads to a competitive climate, whereas recognising the other party's qualities rather leads to a cooperation climate.

Case studies

Use the time variable to influence the climate

US

In the United States, it is not unusual to start meetings at 8 a.m. It is not perceived as hard, as may be the case, for example, in Italy. On the other hand, starting a meeting later, at 9.30 for example, or earlier, at 7.30, sends a message. Starting a meeting early in the morning is often perceived as a sign of competitiveness, while starting a meeting slightly later is rather perceived as a willingness to collaborate.

Use the time variable to influence the climate

AT   UK   SE   AU   CA   US   TR   ZA   EG

In Austria, in the United Kingdom, in Sweden, in Australia, in Canada and in the United States, the informal space is restricted and interpersonal distance is relatively developed. Standing too close to somebody will lead the other party to feel uncomfortable.

In contrast, in Turkey, in Saudi Arabia and in Egypt, the informal space is more developed and the interpersonal distance is relatively limited. Standing close to somebody is very common, while stepping back is considered inappropriate or even, in some cases, insulting.

The way space is used can make the other party comfortable or, alternatively, uncomfortable.

Impact of the concept of present on the negotiation climate

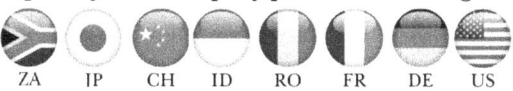
ZA   JP   CH   ID   RO   FR   DE   US

In Saudi Arabia, like in Japan, China, Indonesia and Romania, presents are an integral part of the business culture. However, this is not the case in countries like France, Germany or the United States. Failure to respect the current rules in this area would have an impact on the general negotiation climate.

A present is usually something positive. It is interesting to note how offering a present actually influences the climate and, above all, how the way that present is offered influences the final result!

Saudi Arabia

In Saudi Arabia, only close friends exchange gifts. Making a present to a Saudi Arabian before having formed close relations is likely to make him feel uncomfortable. When you make a present, it is common to make a very good one. Given that Saudi businessmen are often very rich, presents will often cost several thousand euros. The gift will be opened in front of the person who made it and carefully examined by the person who received it in the presence of everyone. This is a proof of respect. Traditionally, gold jewellery and silk garments are reserved to women. Oriental carpets, silver or platinum jewellery, incense or perfume are common gifts for men. Note as well that it is inappropriate for a man to make a gift to a Saudi woman. The present must be offered by another woman.

Japan

In Japan, the gifts ceremony is more important than the gift itself. Gifts can be simple or extravagant. In business environments, presents are often offered during the first meeting or at the end of the year. It is recommended to let your Japanese colleagues offer their present(s) first, so that you can offer them something of the same level. You should know that the Japanese usually do not open their presents in public. If they do, do not be surprised if they react reservedly. It does not mean they don't like their present. It is recommended to wrap up the present in Japan so that the packaging matches local tastes. The best choice is rice-coloured wrapping. White (colour of death) or black wrappings should be avoided. You should also avoid making a present made up of an even number of components. Some examples of appreciated business presents: Imported alcoholic drinks, electronic gadgets, toys for the partners' children or even branded goods.

China

In China, presents are a sensitive subject. Even if it is often against the Chinese law, this practice is widespread. Avoid making valuable presents in front of other people, as this may cause embarrassment. Making a present from your company to a Chinese company is acceptable. Do point out though that it is a present from your company to the whole group. Make sure the present is acknowledged by the leader of the Chinese delegation. Some presents usually appreciated: a banquet, high quality pens, stamps, electronic gadgets from your country, etc. Quality liqueurs and culinary specialties are also appreciated. Do not bring a present containing food at a party or dinner, as this may imply that the food provided is not enough. You should rather send this present after the meeting as a gesture of thanks. Avoid making presents with white, black or blue as main colours. Do not wrap up presents before going through customs, as they are likely to be opened. Moreover, it is better to go for a locally appreciated wrapping. For instance, red is a lucky colour. Rose and yellow are appreciated joyful colours. Presents are always made once the meeting is over. During the Chinese New Year, it is common to offer money (New Year's bonus) to children and to the service staff who regularly help out. The money is usually put in a red envelope. This present is called hong bao. Many employers offer the equivalent of one month's salary "New Year's Day presents" to their employees.

Indonesia

Making presents is part of the Indonesian culture. Any occasion is good to celebrate and make a present: returning home, the arrival of a visitor… The presents may be small but they are certainly exchanged frequently. The presents are not opened in front of the people who offer them. Usually, the person who receives the present thanks you briefly and puts it aside. Opening a present immediately suggests impatience. Moreover, in case the present is not appreciated, that would be embarrassing for everybody. Food is often an appreciated present. The Indonesian Muslims consider dogs to be impure. Avoid making presents which, in one way or another, are related to dogs. Pets like cats and birds are usually appreciated by the Indonesians. Therefore, presents relating to these animals are a good choice for pet lovers. Personal presents from a man to a woman can be interpreted as romantic. It is therefore essential, when a stranger makes a gift to an Indonesian woman, to make clear that the present is offered by his company or even by his wife.

Romania

Presents are part of business in Romania. Significant presents are made on special occasions, such as Christmas, or when a contract is signed. It is nonetheless a good idea to have small presents with the company logo for meetings of all types. A present from your country can also be appreciated.

France

In business, it is recommended not to make presents at the first meeting. Avoid too expensive or too cheap presents. Presents showing a cultural interest are always welcome. A thick and complex book may be a good choice. Simplicity is not particularly valued in France. One should usually write to the other party in order to thank him/her quickly after receiving a present.

Germany

In business, the Germans don't make presents systematically. They do not expect to receive presents either. If you wish to make a present, it is recommended to choose one of excellent quality but of reasonable value. Do not make presents such as perfume or clothes as these are considered as too personal. Scarves are an exception. A quality liqueur or wine from your country is a good present. You should also know state representatives are not allowed to accept presents. Corporate gifts are usually made at Christmas. Nevertheless, an increasing number of German companies content themselves with sending cards or calendars.

United States

Making presents is not an integral part of the business culture. Presents symbolise an emotional affection. They are often exchanged at Christmas or on special occasions such as the retirement of a colleague. The law does not encourage business presents. It is usual to send postcards to customers and colleagues at the end of December, for Christmas or for Hanukkhah. Presents are usually opened immediately and in public. Do not necessarily expect direct reciprocity when it comes to presents.

For women, presents like perfume or clothes are appropriate in the business environment. Offering presents to children may be a good idea, but you must make sure to respect the parents' beliefs. Typical objects from your country or electronic gadgets can be a good choice of present.

Managing the negotiation stages

The majority of negotiations follow a pattern made up of six sequential stages. The ability to identify these stages is particularly important in order to take decisions linked to the negotiation rhythm, the time of investigations, the introduction of strategies, etc. Experienced negotiators are aware of these stages and take them into account while planning their strategies. Each stage must be fully developed in order to make the most of the negotiation.

3. The keys to a successful intercultural negotiation

Table 3.5. Summary of the negotiation stages

	Definition
Preparation stage	Data gathering and identification of potential problems.
Introduction stage	The parties establish the framework and develop their relations through the establishment of common ground.
Differentiation stage	The parties examine their differences, present their points of view and define the conflict zone.
Integration stage	The parties develop and check the possible options. It is also the stage where they look for alternative solutions which may resolve the problems and lead to the conclusion of an agreement.
Setting up stage	The parties present their final offers and make commitments.
Follow-up stage	The parties lay the foundations of their future relations.

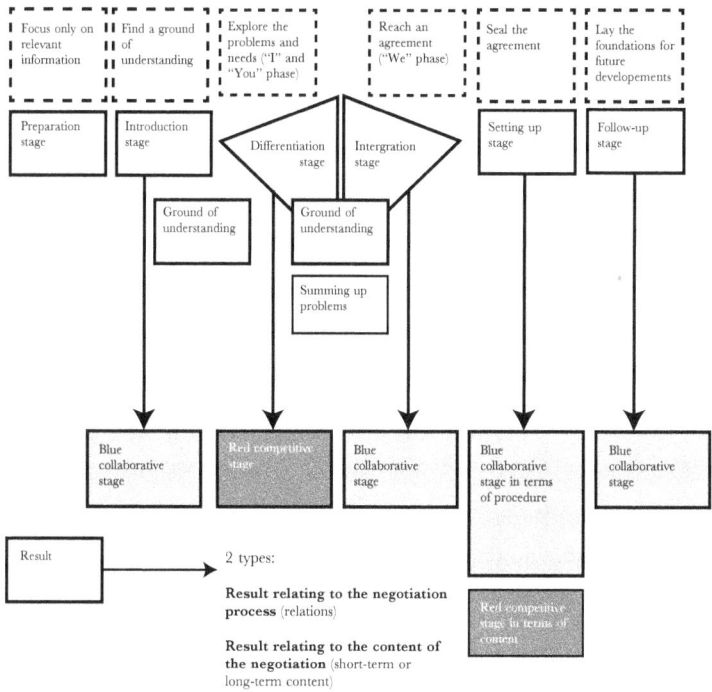

Figure 3.4.

Table 3.6

	Objectives
Preparation stage	• Gather all relevant information which can be used during the negotiation process. • Identify problems and sources of potential synergies.
Introduction stage	• Establish the framework (general presentation and starting discussions). • Establish common ground (on a personal or organisational level). • Develop a favourable negotiation climate (by focusing on what is positive). • Make sure all parties have a real understanding of the subject at hand. • Reach agreements on elements of the negotiation process such as basic rules in force, timing, behaviour…
Differentiation stage	• Begin negotiations. Who will make the first step? • Manage conflicts in the aim of exploring differences. • Share your emotions. • Keep to the organisational level when discussing differences and avoid personal conflicts. • Break potential deadlocks by identifying the parties' underlying needs. • Make sure the differentiation has been completed before going further. • Avoid making concessions on content at this stage.
Integration stage	• Change style, if necessary, to adapt to the other party. • Possibly influence the negotiation climate. • Put forward areas of agreement and the common ground already established. • Change level (switch from organisational to personal level and vice versa). • Promote the other party's self-esteem. • Focus the other parties' attention on the future, not the past.

Integration stage (contd)	• Encourage the parties to look for solutions rather than problems. • Seek options (to this end, use the power of asking questions). • Use the most cooperative member(s) of the other party as vector of evolution. • Stress the importance of reaching an agreement and underline the possible long-term consequences in case of failure to reach an agreement. • Review the negotiation process and determine which lever(s) would lead to a satisfactory result. • Start exchanging concessions on content.
Setting up stage	• Summarize the situation focusing on the common ground. • Make clear and specific final offers. • Get an agreement in principle in case the other party there present does not have final decision power. • Develop mechanisms (personal and organizational) to implement the agreement. • Draw up the terms of the agreement. • Consider the development of procedures setting conflicts.
Follow-up stage	• Build bridges for the future development of relations.

	Behaviour
Preparation stage	• Focus on facts, not on opinions.
Introduction stage	• Be rather informal. The idea is to meet, discuss and socialise. • One person usually takes the lead in the discussions.
Differentiation stage	• Make assertions. • Detail your expectations and problems. • Often use non-verbal language. • Ask open questions.

Integration stage	• Get usually closer to the negotiations' table. • Look for balance. • Make concessions on both sides. • Make sure to keep a favourable position, or even a dominant one. • Use hypothetical questions to find solutions. • Investigate options. • Use many different tactics in order to achieve the final objective.
Setting up stage	• Summarise a number of elements and facts (often coming from all kinds of reports). • Seal the agreement.
Follow-up stage	• Make sure you stay in contact. • Keep an open mind.

Case Studies

Planning of a negotiation

IN

For Indians, the expression: "time is money" does not mean anything. Expect delays as they are unavoidable most of the time. In India, the approach to time is different than in the Western world. It is recommended to adopt a realistic attitude in terms of the negotiation stages planning. It is essential to take this aspect into consideration in the management of the negotiation stages.

Rhythm of negotiation in Mexico, Argentina and Brazil versus rhythm of negotiation in the United States

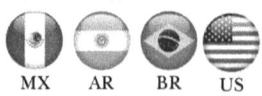
MX   AR   BR   US

In Mexico, Argentina and Brazil the negotiating rhythm is rather slow. People take time to know each other before doing business. This is less the case in the United States, where the business rhythm is particularly fast. In major American companies, it is not unusual for a manager to approve a contract worth 10.000 dollars in a single meeting.

Rhythm of negotiations in Germany and Belgium

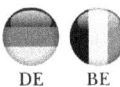
DE   BE

In Germany, the decision making process is rather slow as many participants come into consideration. Once the decision is made, it is definite, even "irrevocable". The decision making process is very methodical. You should know that in addition to the official command chain German organisations usually have a parallel set of consultants and decision-makers. This "secret cabinet's" approval is often compulsory. At each stage, the details of the offer are carefully analyzed. Do not try to speed up the negotiation process. In some respects, the Germans consider that to do things well, they should take their time.

In Belgium, the decision process is also slow, as several external participants are part of the process and must be consulted. Let us remind that this is related to the country's diversity.

Planning of a negotiation

ZA   SE   UK

The prevailing managerial logic influences time management and, as a consequence, the planning of negotiation stages. Let us take the example of Saudi Arabia, Sweden and the United Kingdom.

Saudi Arabia has a managerial logic rather based on honour. As a result, much time is dedicated to building relations with the participants. This process corresponds to the introduction stage.

The managerial logic in Sweden is rather based on the search for consensus. Much time is dedicated to establishing a common ground between participants. This corresponds to the differentiation and integration stages.

In the United Kingdom, the managerial logic is based on contracts. Much time is dedicated to defining the terms of the agreement, which corresponds to the setting up stage.

Rhythm of negotiations in Poland and the United States

In Poland, the negotiation rhythm is rather slow. Concluding a business agreement may take some time as the Poles are usually very careful. Therefore, it can take months to sign a contract. Fast moves often make entrepreneurs rather anxious.

In contrast, in the United States, the level of tolerance to uncertainty is rather high and the rhythm of business is very fast.

Remaining in the negotiation zone

The negotiation zone is the space within which all parties have an interest to negotiate (figure 3.5). You must make sure not to leave this zone as, once out, it may prove difficult to find your way back in.

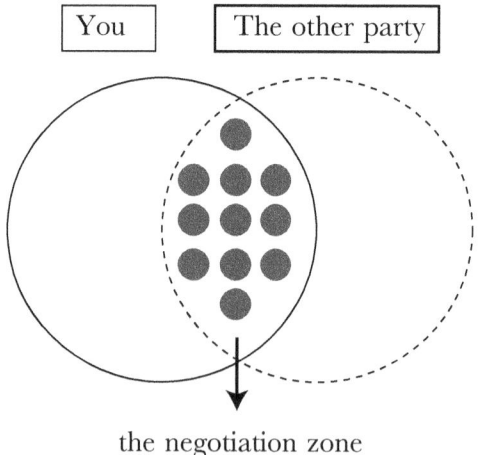

Figure 3.5 – Negotiation zone

Proactively consider a fallback option – BATNA/MESORE

The term "fallback option" has a negative connotation to the extent that it implicitly refers to a failure situation. Fisher and Ury[11], negotiation specialists of Harvard University, have suggested the term "BATNA" – "Best Alternative To a Negotiated Agreement". (Note the French equivalent is "MESORE" – "MEilleures Solutions de REchange"). This new terminology has the advantage of dropping the notion of failure. If you are unable to reach an agreement, the idea is to find another solution. In that way, this approach is constructive and enables to get the negotiations back on course.

▸ **Why is a fallback option necessary?**

Three arguments must be put forward:
- *having a safeguard:* a person without a fallback option is of course more inclined to make concessions to conclude a business negotiation, sometimes beyond what is reasonable.
- *having an assessment "barometer":* a fallback option enables you to assess when the interest of a negotiation strongly declines, or even when the negotiation stops being interesting at all. If the negotiated solution is less profitable than the fallback option, ask yourself whether you should go ahead with the negotiation. On the other hand, if the negotiated solution is more profitable than the fallback option, this is a good sign. The fallback option is a reference to avoid concluding an unfavourable agreement or missing a favourable one. It is necessary to remind that the purpose of negotiation is to reach a better result than what would be the case without it. If it is not the case, it is pointless to waste time!
- *enhancing self-confidence:* having a fallback option gives confidence during the negotiation.

▸ **How to prepare a fallback option**

Fisher and Ury recommend a three-step approach:
1. Think of several possible fallback options;
2. Focus on the three or four most interesting options and determine how to put them into practice;
3. Choose the most satisfactory option.

Considering several options is a beneficial process which requires creativity. It opens the field by making you consider the situation from different angles. It also makes you ask the good questions.

---

11 Fischer R., Ury W., *Getting to Yes. Negotiating Agreement Without Giving In*, Guernsey, Arrow Edition, 1987.

It is essential to consider the feasibility of several alternative options. You can only talk of fallback solution when you have a specific idea of the way you will develop it and of its actual cost. At this stage, it is important not to keep it vague and to go by specific and verified facts.

> **A fallback option is not a negotiation threshold**

Traditionally, the negotiation threshold is the point above which, or alternatively below which, you refuse to go. This threshold enables the negotiator to control some driftings of the negotiation and to stop if s/he enters a critical zone. Nevertheless, given its radical aspect, the negotiation threshold is likely to block somehow the negotiation. It may crystallise the positions and make the exchanges fruitless.

The negotiation threshold is a useful tool if properly used, i.e. more as an indicator than as a threshold. On the other hand, it is recommended to always keep one's fallback option in mind, as it can be used as a reference in order to assess the other party's proposals.

Breaking the deadlock

In negotiation, it is rather usual to reach a deadlock. This does not usually happen intentionally.

Reactions to be avoided when reaching a deadlock: Tell the other party his/her perceptions are wrong; ask him/her to adopt another point of view; put pressure on the other party in order to have your point of view accepted, threaten him/her or even make negative comments on the individuals. All these would only worsen the situation.

In case of a deadlock, it is useless to strengthen your positions, as that would only widen the gap between the parties. At this stage, it is important not to make concessions on content with the aim of breaking the deadlock. This line of action would reward the other party for the deadlock and would encourage it to reproduce the same situation in the future in order to get more concessions from you.

When looking closely at deadlocks, we realise they are more often connected to procedural problems, i.e. relations and people, than to content. For example, the personal needs of an individual might have not been satisfied. To break the deadlock, it is recommended not to focus on the content and to analyze the situation from a broader perspective.

> ### Three-step method to break the deadlock
>
> **1. Identify the specific needs of the other party that have not been satisfied.**
>
> - Re-examine the other party's needs: individual needs versus organisational needs and expressed needs versus hidden needs.
>
> **2. Stop talking about the deadlock content and review the process.**
>
> - Check the way the negotiation is managed. For example: identify the other party's negotiation style, assess the influence of your behaviour on the other party, identify how the negotiation climate is controlled, assess the parties' level of trust…
>
> **3. Change the process.**
>
> - Adapt the process so that the other party feels the negotiation goes in the right direction. Make sure nobody loses face, particularly to the extent that a change of process does not mean a change of content. Breaking the deadlock requires imagination and creativity.

Here is a non-exhaustive list including four categories of tactics that can be used in order to break the deadlock. These are tactics aiming at improving the environment, the relations, the ways to proceed and the elements of content.

▶ **Tactics to improve the environment**

Suggest to the parties to continue discussions in separate rooms in order to consider everyone's position. In return, it is recommended to be the first to ask for the suggestions of the other party.

▶ **Tactics to improve relations**

1. Take a "recreational" break. For example, suggesting to have a cold drink reduces stress.

2. Leave the formal framework. Suggest leaving the formal negotiation framework in order to discuss the problem face-to-face, without taking any notes.
3. Call upon positive memories. Remind the successful collaboration of the parties in the past and, eventually, how the parties managed to go beyond their differences. Based on these memories, you can ask the other party how in their opinion you could do the same at present.
4. Create associations with the future or the past. Establish a connection between the current need of breaking the deadlock and past positive results for the other party or future projects and needs.
5. Change the negotiators. Modify the negotiation team, for example, by replacing former members or adding new ones. You may even suggest to the other party to follow the same line.
6. Show empathy. Use the power of asking questions.

▸ **Tactics to improve the ways to proceed**

1. Remind the objectives of the negotiation. The negotiation is carried out for a reason and all parties must keep this in mind. Reaffirm the need to find a win-win solution and make reference to the common ground.
2. Summarise and confirm the areas of agreement. Summarising frequently the details of the common ground and the points on which an agreement has already been found is a very efficient tactic. It is recommended to frequently reaffirm your adherence to these points of agreement.
3. Consider the problems from different perspectives. By redefining the problem this can lead to a step-by-step review (breaking down the problem in smaller parts) or, alternatively, to a reconstruction (combining different elements in an unexpected or unusual way in order to make up a whole that is easier to approach).
4. Consider the future consequences of a failure. Consider together favourable and unfavourable consequences in case of non-conclusion of the agreement.
5. Ask a hypothetical question. Put the other party's state of mind to the test and assess the extent to which s/he would be willing to make a move to break the deadlock by asking hypothetical questions: "What would happen if...?"
6. Encourage the other party to consider another perspective. For example, suggest to the other party to imagine what s/he would do if s/he were in your shoes.
7. Reexamine the negotiation process. Agree on a method or on tools to be used in order to break the deadlock.

8. Have a sense of humour. Introducing some humour (cracking a joke or showing self-derision, for example) may ease the emotional climate of the negotiation.
9. Change the timing or the venue of the negotiation. These variables are relatively easy to control and they have a strong influence on the negotiation climate.
10. Try to draw a very quick conclusion. Make a positive proposal which the other party would find difficult to refuse or refute.
11. Use brainstorming in order to draw up a list of options to break the deadlock. Using a white board for this exercise can positively influence the negotiation climate as it focuses participants' attention on a specific object.
12. Establish a study committee. Suggest presenting the subject to a committee or "reflection group" made up of representative members of the different parties and set a deadline for the committee's report on the given subject.
13. Call upon an authority. Request the opinion of a third party, such as a renowned expert. You could decide to consider this third voice as a source of advice or even as a "rule" to apply.
14. Call upon a mediator.
15. Suggest arbitration.

▶ **Tactics to improve elements of content**

1. Introduce new elements: For example, present new information enabling the parties to consider the subject from a different perspective.
2. Make a conditional offer. Make an offer to the other party provided that s/he will do something in return.
3. Look for foundation stones on which you could capitalise: link conflicting points of view to a third point in order to bridge different opinions.
4. Concentrate on remaining alternatives. Suggest picking one and enforcing it for a period of probation.

Case studies

What to do when there is no trust?

SE   AU

In that case, it is essential to identify the source factors of trust and to use them. Staying in the negotiation zone is mainly a question of trust.

In Sweden, for example, punctuality is respected and valued. Meetings are supposed to start and finish on time. Missing a deadline without good reason is considered as a proof of incompetence or, at least, as a proof of your incapacity to efficiently manage your time. It is the same in Australia. It is therefore essential to respect deadlines. Consequently, being punctual is a good way of creating trust.

Rules, values, value orientation and negotiation zone

UA   RO   BR

In Ukraine, as in Romania or in Brazil, the notion of prestige is important and inspires trust. Therefore, it is recommended to stay in prestigious hotels when visiting those countries. All aspects of yourself and of your "circle" must reflect prestige.

Organisation and negotiation zone

TR

In Turkey, various topics of conversation are appreciated: Turkish history (avoid focusing on conflicts), tourism, cultural achievements, sports (wrestling is a very popular sport). If you are talking to a father, talking about his family is usually a source of pride. The notion of family is a factor of trust in Turkey. It is important that these elements be reflected in your speech.

Adapting the language used

Communication is a dynamic process through which information is exchanged among several individuals by means of a common system of symbols, signs and behaviours. The parties must therefore have a common language. It is important to adapt your language to the one used by the other party.

Communication model

There are a lot of communication models aiming at explaining the process of communication. Claude Shannon and Warren Weaver's model[12] was selected for the following reasons (figure 3.6): it is simple to understand and easy to activate. It was initially a linear model in which communication was reduced to its simplest terms: the transmission of a message. An information source sends an encoded message to a receiver which decodes it.

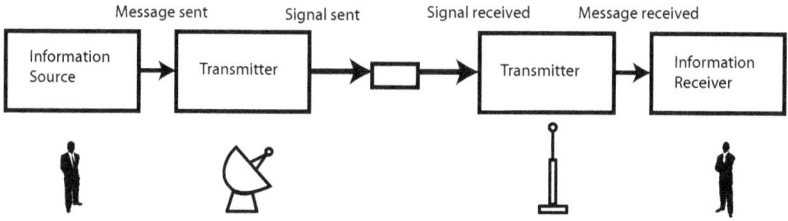

Figure 3.6 – Shannon & Weaver's initial model

This model had two major flaws: it was unidirectional and did not explain the potential differences in meaning between the message emitted by the source and the final message that is received.

Shannon and Weaver introduced two additional concepts to their communication model (figure 3.7):
- noise: all elements (culture, mood of the moment, economic situation, etc.) which may interfere with the transmission of information;
- feedback: the feedback makes the system multidirectional.

---

12 Claude E. Shannon and Warren Weaver, *A Mathematical Theory of Communication*, University of Illinois Press, 1949.

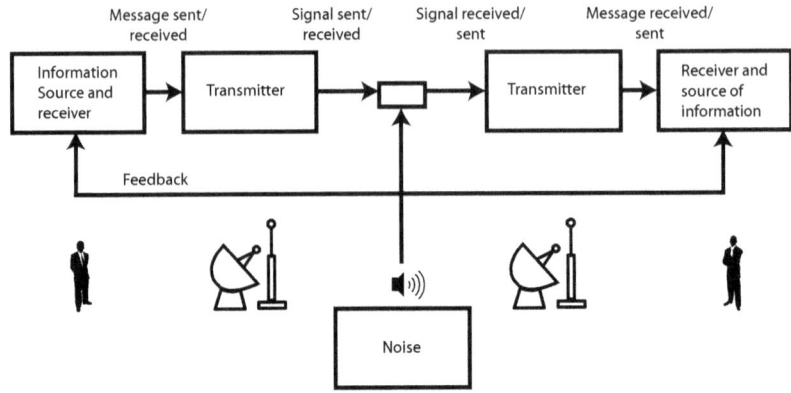

Figure 3.7 – Shannon & Weaver's adapted model

It is essential to determine which type of negotiation is expected and to assess the importance of verbal, non-verbal and para-verbal communication.

Case studies

Language adaptation and choice of arguments put forward

The United States, Canada, Australia and the United Kingdom are usually short-term oriented nations. The individuals are anxious about getting results or about the capacity to produce something in time. Taking this element into consideration and including it in our reasoning is usually effective. Use words like "short-term benefits" or "fast progress".

Language adaptation and choice of arguments put forward

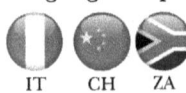

In Italy, family is essential. Historically, Italy was made up of different regions, each with their own dialect, political life and culture. These regions were frequently at war. For this reason, family life became a principal concern.

The leitmotiv "family comes first" reflects the need for Italians to protect themselves, their families as well as their culture. This means that the notion of family must be included in your arguments. Use words like "group interest" or "unity". This is also the case in China, where family is often the foundation of society. In Saudi Arabia, the process is rather similar. Belonging to a tribe, to a family is still the cornerstone of an individual's social identity.

SE

In Sweden, the concepts of egalitarianism, neutrality, relaxation and respect for humanity and nature are of fundamental importance. Make sure this is reflected in your language and approach.

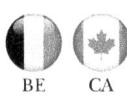
BE   CA

Belgium has a rather stability-oriented culture. In contrast, the culture in Canada is rather change-oriented. It is important to use arguments reflecting the tendencies of the environment, without of course lapsing into stigmatisation.

ES

Religious, national and other ideologies are very important in Spain and can be used as the cornerstone of an argument.

Spain is a very catholic country. Although there is no official religion in Spain, more than 90% of the Spanish are, in a way, practising Catholics. A vast majority of the Spanish people, practising or not, are familiar with the basic principles of the Catholic Church. Catholicism is source of stability.

The principle according to which all men are equal and each individual is unique is of fundamental importance. It can also be used as the cornerstone of an argument.

DE   AT   UK   US   CA   AU

In the following countries (Germany, Austria, the United Kingdom, the United States, Canada, Australia) real and established facts are "source of truth". People rely on these as a priority. Of course, this does not prevent personal feelings from being taken into consideration at one moment or another. In case of conflict, concrete facts and scientific data take precedence over all the rest. So, it is essential that your arguments include concrete facts and not impressions or assumptions.

Using the power of listening and asking questions

Verbal communication includes speech and the ability to listen. Moreover, decisions are based on what we hear and observe or, more precisely, on what we think we hear and observe. The ability to listen is a power. Of course, blockages may arise during the listening process.

Main sources of blockage

- Making assumptions leading to false conclusions.
- Interrupting the other party before s/he has finished presenting his/her opinions and remarks.
- Being firm without taking into account views that could be contrary to yours.
- Listening selectively, while discarding the points we do not wish to hear.
- Being too critical towards the other party.
- Letting your judgment be distorted by personal opinions or by such elements as somebody's appearance.
- Not showing much respect to the other party and showing that you have the feeling of being better than s/he is.
- Being afraid of the influence the other party may have on you.

- Being worried about other subjects not related to the negotiation (such as personal matters).
- Speaking too much (some negotiators seem to feel they have to speak a lot during negotiations in order to justify their presence and participation).
- Using technical terminology with which the other parties are not acquainted.
- etc.

The average human brain is capable of processing between 600 and 800 words per minute, while a speech only contains between 100 and 300 words. This fact leaves a significant margin to the brain to divide attention to other matters while listening to a conversation.

Active listening

Actively listening to the other party has many advantages: you save time for your answers; it compels you to process the captured information and shows to the other party that you understand their views, in full or in part.

Active listening needs three successive processes: remaining neutral, demonstrating your attention and confirming your understanding:

- remaining neutral implies that you listen to the other party without judging, be it positively or negatively. It also means that you should put yourself in the other party's shoes ("In what sense is this important for the other party?") and distinguish facts from emotions and impressions;
- demonstrating your attention implies that you show in a verbal manner (using words and phrases like "mmm", "I see" or "really") as well as in a non-verbal manner (for example, by smiling or nodding) that you follow the conversation. This also means that you encourage the other party to continue (using sentences like "tell me more" or "go on, please");
- confirming your understanding can be achieved in various ways: e.g. by using reflective questions or summarising techniques. The aim of course is to confirm your understanding and not to give your consent. You must not only demonstrate your understanding of the facts, but also of the expressed emotions.

Looking for the real meaning of words and avoiding the use of emotional phrases: You have to distinguish the real meaning of words (what is said in the figurative and literal sense) from their hidden meaning (what is meant by using certain words rather than others, what the voice pitch indicates...). Experienced negotiators make sure that they discover the real meaning of words and avoid using irritating or emotional sentences. For example: "In my humble opinion..."; "As you know very well..."; "To be fully honest..."; "I see what you are saying, but..."; "With all due respect..."; "Do not take this too seriously..."; "I do not wish to judge you, but..."; "I am just being reasonable and honest..."...

Some words bring about conflict (competitive or red words) or, alternatively, create an atmosphere of collaboration (collaborative or blue words) (table 3.7). It is also useful to employ the other party's key words (when developing arguments or drafting reports).

Table 3.7 – Examples of competitive or collaborative key words

Competitive words	Behaviour
Problem	Situation, subject, point...
Annoying	Remarkable, interesting, unusual...
Negotiate	Discuss, suggest, recommend...
You	We, together, jointly...
Must	We could, it might, maybe...
...	....

The power of asking questions

Well-formulated questions are very powerful negotiation tools. Asking the right questions enables negotiating parties to keep the negotiation process under control. A "good question" can enumerate facts, validate assumptions, satisfy the other party's needs, etc.

Experienced negotiators prepare their questions carefully. The preparation level of questions is an indicator of the general preparation level of the negotiation. Sometimes the other party may feel reluctant to answer certain questions. Explaining why we ask such questions or exchanging information in return reduces the other party's "anxiety".

▶ **Questions types**

There are many ways to classify questions according to their structure or use. Let us consider five types of fundamental questions in negotiation:
- *Open questions:* Open questions extend the dialogue. These are questions that cannot be answered by "yes" or "no". Here are some examples: "What do you think of...?"; "What does this mean to you...?"
- *Closed questions:* closed questions call for simple and factual answers. These are questions that can usually be answered by "yes" or "no".
- *Reflective questions:* the idea is to paraphrase what the other party said. These paraphrases include the key words used by the other party. For example, start with "So, are you saying that...?" or "So, do you think that...?". Make sure you stay neutral and do not add elements to the summary.
- *Hypothetical questions:* Hypothetical questions are very useful in negotiation, as they lead the other party to consider options and alternatives. They make it possible to "see how the land lies". They usually start with: "What would we do if...?" or "Let us assume that...?". Through their structure (they reflect possibilities and not established facts) hypothetical questions offer the advantage of not putting the other party into a position of wanting to strongly argue about something.
- *Directive questions:* These are targeted and oriented questions leading the negotiator where he wants to.

Points to consider when preparing your questions:
- What kind of questions should I ask? Simple questions are usually the best ones.
- How should I ask my questions? The impact on the climate has to be taken into account.
- When should I ask my questions? You must carefully choose the right moment.

▶ **Purposes of asking questions**

Here is a non-exhaustive list of purposes for which you may ask questions:
- *Drawing attention:* Experienced negotiators use questions to lead the other party to expose his opinions more thoroughly. Examples of sentences that can be used for this purpose: "How are you? " ; "May I ask you a question?" ; "Nice day isn't it?"...
- *Obtaining or verifying information:* when seeking information, it is recommended to juggle with open and closed questions. Open

questions enable you to better understand the situation, whereas closed questions enable you to clarify it.
- *Starting the reflection:* Questions can be used to stimulate reflection of the other party and lead him/her to share opinions. You can use fully opened questions, such as "How do you think we should proceed?" or resort to more targeted questions, such as: "What do you suggest regarding…?" or: "What are the advantages of…?".
- *Confirming your understanding:* Reflective questions are particularly effective in showing the other party that you understood his/her point of view. If the reflective question is correct, the other party shall agree and will be encouraged to provide you with more details about his opinions.
- *Providing information:* you can ask questions implying the answer, such as "as an experienced director you surely are already considering…?". It is recommended to be careful with "negatively formulated" informative questions, like "How can you consider this idea worthless?" because such questions can lead the other party to be on the defensive.
- *Suggesting options or alternatives:* a hypothetical declaration followed by an opened question is a good strategy to suggest options. For example: "I read in the newspaper that… in what way does this seem relevant to you?". Even if the other party runs down the idea, this strategy gives you the opportunity to get going thanks to another opened question, such as "I do not either entirely agree with what the author of the article says, but I am still wondering about the points raised that could be relevant".
- *Leading the other party to a conclusion:* once the parties have enough information and have had the chance to sufficiently discuss it, the use of reflective questions can help concluding the negotiation. Some examples of reflective questions: "Isn't it about time to…?" or: "Do you prefer x or y?"

The importance of answers

Knowing how to answer a question is as important as knowing how to ask it. The art of answering questions does not necessarily depend on the fact of being right or wrong. It is rather about knowing when to be clear and when to be ambiguous.

You may not want to answer a question straight away or might wish to prevent the other party from asking this particular question. The following strategies can be useful in these cases:
- answering in part or without going straight to the point: "I see the situation in such way…";

- re-orientating the question: "I'd rather ask…";
- broadening the question: "Let me add that…";
- dividing the question in several parts: "There are several aspects to be taken into consideration. Firstly…";
- changing perspective: "From the company's point of view… However, in a national perspective…";
- providing optional answers: "On the one hand… and on the other hand…";
- stating that the question is inappropriate or untimely: "It would be inappropriate from me to answer…";
- changing the subject: "Very interesting question. It reminds me of…";
- providing an "open" answer: "You could be wrong but you could be right as well";
- asking another question in return: "What does interest you in…";
- blocking: "That's a good question. I'll have to think about it, before I answer you";
- leaving the question unanswered: Promise to answer another time or to another person;
- stating that the question is hypothetical or based on false or incomplete information: "Your question is based on an old report and therefore does not reflect the current situation";
- showing your sense of humour and laugh at the question. This strategy should be used in moderation and good judgment;
- pretending you do not understand: "Could you please repeat the question ?";
- saying nothing and using silence;
- etc.

The power of silence

A lot of negotiators are not comfortable with silence and feel the need to "fill in the blanks". Silence may prove to be a very efficient tactic. For example, silence may urge the negotiating party to answer the question he himself asked. In general, it is recommended to introduce silent breaks through the communication process. This allows you to slow down the negotiation rhythm and gives the other party the impression you take his point of view into account and the negotiation seriously.

Case studies

How is information absorbed?

AT

Austrians usually absorb information in a structured manner. Their approach to negotiation is rather slow and one-dimensional. Note that it is important to be ready for every meeting and be able to provide the necessary facts and figures.

How is information absorbed?

FR CH

A French colleague is complaining: "The Chinese teams never do what we ask. It's hard to work with them. Yet, we sent them all the reports. They are informed about everything." When s/he is asked the following question: "Do you regularly meet your Chinese colleagues?" s/he answers: "They spent three months in France at the beginning of the project; we should know each other by now. Spending more money on traveling is out of the question."

At this advanced stage of the project, it is essential to avoid reinforcing existing stereotypes about the other culture: The French concur that the Chinese people do exactly as they please, despite the fact that they have been provided with all the information, and the Chinese keep on thinking that the French people neither collaborate nor communicate with them.

The different perceptions related to the use of oral or written communication have an important impact on the way business should be managed. The most impressive impact lies in the magnitude these differences can reach in case of conflict. The power of listening and asking questions is essential at this stage.

Conclusion

Experienced negotiators use the six keys of the SNA tool, whether instinctively or after having learned them. These are rules or principles enabling the negotiators to highly increase their chances of success in a negotiation. Here is a brief assessment of these principles:

- "using the balance of powers" allows negotiators to reinforce their perceived position, no matter what their real position is;
- rules such as "managing the negotiation climate", "remaining in the negotiation zone" or "adapting the language" allow the negotiators, amongst other things, to manage the negotiation process and go from difficult situations to positive and successful ones;
- the majority of negotiations respect a plan including six sequential phases. Each phase must be fully developed in order to achieve a good negotiation result. This is "managing the negotiation phases". As negotiators, we have to identify these phases and prepare ourselves accordingly;
- listening to the other party is a key part of communication. Unfortunately, this component is forgotten far too often. "Using the power of listening and asking questions" is probably one of the best pieces of advice you could receive in negotiation.

CHAPTER 4

HOW TO PREPARE THE NEGOTIATION

"Man is born to live, not to prepare for life."
Boris Pasternak

Subject: Identify the essential elements on which we must concentrate before starting the negotiation, so that it develops in the best possible way.

This first quote could at first sight seem provocative in a chapter about preparation. And yet, it isn't... Luck favours the well prepared! However, it is important to keep in mind that this stage, like all the others, must lead to action and results. So, it is recommended to be well prepared; however, a long "over-analysis" should be avoided. This chapter considers the preparation of a negotiation in stages:

- how to establish contacts in business?
- how to identify the negotiating parties?
- how to identify the negotiators' objectives, determine the negotiation threshold and find common ground?
- how to identify what influences and motivates the negotiating parties?
- choosing a negotiating style and identifying the style of the other party;
- analyzing the situation;
- organising the meeting.

How to establish contacts in business

In order to identify how to establish contact with an individual, we must consider two elements: the best way and the best time to establish contact with somebody.

There are multiple ways of establishing contact with somebody. It can be done by direct contact (as in the case of Sweden) or by indirect contact (as in the case of Russia, where using local intermediaries is of vital importance).

- Is it necessary to be introduced by a member of the community?

- Are there particular communication protocols that should be observed?
- Is it necessary to create bonds before the negotiation?
- How should information be transmitted to the right people?

Choosing the time of introductions is a facilitating element. So, in China for example, people attach great importance to the notion of luck. This means that choosing a day believed to be auspicious for introducing yourself could be appreciated.

Respecting the habits and customs in force is a golden rule. All these elements must be considered beforehand.

Case studies

Establishing contact in China, the importance of the notion of guanxi in China

CH

Guanxi[13] is a Chinese concept referring to relations or a network of contacts. It describes the basic dynamic of the personal networks of influence and plays a principal role in the Chinese society.

This Chinese term is broadly used in order to refer to its two usual translations (connection and network of contacts). However, neither of these could correctly reflect the broad cultural implications conveyed by the term guanxi.

The term describes a personal relationship between two individuals in which one of them can ask the other to help him/her out or do him/her a favour, and vice versa. In guanxi, these two individuals do not need to come from the same level or social environment.

Guanxi can also be a network of contacts an individual can call upon when s/he needs something to be done and in which s/he may have influence on behalf of somebody else.

---

13 Source : http://zeblog.majest.net/guanxi/comment-page-1/

Guanxi also refers to a good understanding and interaction between two people: one of them knows perfectly well what the other expects or needs and will take these elements into consideration in his/her future actions having an impact on the other person (and vice versa as well).

The term guanxi is neither used to describe family relations, nor to describe relations within a defined social network. However, it can derive from these relations (such as relations between employers and employees, teachers and students, friends, etc.) For all that, guanxi can be defined as an extended family, in an intuitu personae relation which is not transferable.

Establishing contact in Germany and Sweden

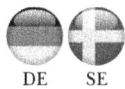

DE   SE

Germany is a country hierarchical distances are significant. It is therefore essential to respect hierarchy when establishing contact. In a country like Sweden, where the hierarchical distance is much lower, this element is of much less importance.

Identifying the parties to the negotiation

You may think that only the parties to a negotiation are the negotiators. In reality, it is not the case, as many other people come into it. You will have to identify who really takes the decisions.

Let us take the example of parents buying a car. The parents take the decision, but the children often strongly influence the final choice.

First, you have to identify who intervenes and how in a negotiation process. Below you will find several categories of parties, for your information:

- *buyers (or payers):* They finance the purchase or the negotiated measure. It is important to know the budgetary as well as the possible levers you may use: settlement periods, payment facilities…;
- *users:* They use the product or service, or benefit from the concluded agreement. They are usually neither involved in the negotiation nor directly affected by the price. Their interests rather lie on the final choice. They may influence the course of the negotiation by means of their

requests. You must know their exact expectations and influence over the negotiation. Sometimes, it is relatively easy to make them your allies;

- *experts:* They are consulted by the negotiating parties on specific aspects of the discussion. They don't directly intervene in the negotiation process. Experts usually have technical and objective opinions and, therefore, there is no reason to try and influence them. On the other hand, you can determine and develop the importance of the analyzed matter in the final decision process. If an expert is consulted in a negotiation, it is in your interest to value an aspect on which their expertise is favourable to you. On the other hand, you should minimise the importance of an aspect on which your proposal will be less interesting than the other party's;

- *opinion leaders:* Opinion leaders help define the needs. They influence the "terms and conditions", i.e. the description of the product or service to be provided or of the agreement to reach. Opinion leaders are usually upstream and sometimes downstream of the negotiation process. In some cases they also take up the role of users, but this is not the rule. Knowing opinion leaders (their expectations, their constraints...) is essential in order to make an appropriate offer to the other party;

- *decision-makers:* They arbitrate between several proposals or formally approve of the actions prepared through the negotiation. In a company, it is not unusual for a contract negotiated for several weeks to be in fine submitted for approval to a manager who has not taken part in the negotiation. You have to assess the decision-makers' level of competence on the subject;

- *negotiators:* these are the people you negotiate with and they only represent the visible part of the iceberg. They can be stakeholders or, alternatively, be commissioned by other players. It is essential to know the nogotiators' level of freedom.

Identify roles rather than people. A single person may have several roles. It is therefore more sensible to consider the roles rather than the people holding them. In order to do that, you should ask yourself the following questions:

- Who negotiates? Is the negotiating party the only person involved in the decision process?
- At the end of discussions, who is going to pay the cost of the object of negotiation?
- Once the agreement has been concluded, who will be affected by or benefit from, the consequences? If you are dealing with products or services, who is going to use them?

- In the decision process, is there a person or a group that must approve the agreement or the negotiated contract?
- Are there people that the negotiating party or the decision-maker should formally consult? In that case, what is the procedure to be followed? How does the opinion of these people influence the decision making process?
- Are there people who may influence the course of negotiations by providing informal advice or whose opinion may influence, for example, the definition of the needs? In that case, what is the type and the extent of their influence?

The analysis of participants is worth to be done, whether you are dealing with a complex negotiation (involving multiple players who do not meet each other) or with a daily negotiation. In every situation, there are many hidden players. Do not underestimate the importance of this analysis that must be carried out in order to visualise the other party's situation as well as our own.

Tool: the influence matrix

The influence matrix allows you to distinguish decision-makers from influential people. In terms of influence, a distinction must be drawn between the influence a person can exert on a given occasion from the cumulative influence this person can have through time.

Table 4.1 – Example of influential people in a typical Belgian family

BE

Importance at a given moment					
50+	The mother-in-law		The Patriarch		
50		The elder brother			
40	The younger brother		The uncle	The family friend	
30					
20			The partner		
10					
	0	25	50	80	100%

Cumulative influence

Case studies

Choice of the negotiating parties, meeting of a Japanese manager with an English manager in the framework of negotiations related to the development of a voice recognition software

JP   UK

The manager of an English SME goes to Japan to discuss directly with one of his suppliers of technical components for a voice recognition software. The other party, a middle-aged sales manager, asks the interpreter where is the manager of the SME. It seems difficult for him to realise that this young man, without white hair, can be the general manager of the customer company. In Japan, older people are highly respected. Age determines the rank on the importance scale. The choice of the negotiators must take this fact into account as much as possible.

Choice of the negotiating parties, meeting of a Japanese manager with an English manager in the framework of negotiations related to the development of a voice recognition software

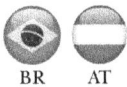

BR   AT

Two R&D companies in the area of bone prosthesis, one located in Brazil and the other one in Austria, have developed complementary technologies. The general managers of these companies decide to organise a meeting in Sao Paolo to discuss a potential partnership.

The meeting takes place at the headquarters of the Brazilian company at 10 a.m. The general managers exchange their views and each of them provides an overall picture of his company, strategies and major projects in hand. The Austrian interlocutor looks interested in the Brazilian presentation, but seems surprised. The presentation of the Brazilian company is interrupted several times, first by a phone call and then by associates entering the office.

Generally speaking, the Austrians are rather monochronic, whereas the Brazilians are much more polychronic. The choice of negotiators must take into account their capacity to adapt to the other party's relation to time.

Choice of a negotiator to go on a specific mission

ES

The Spanish are known for their pride and high sense of honour. They are more proud of strong personal features than of professional capacities. It is important to choose carefully your representative.

DE

When it comes to determining roles according to gender, the German society is rather flexible. Whether you are a man or a woman, the most important is to show self-control and confidence. For that matter, Germany elected a female chancellor at its head in 2009.

Choice of candidates to lead negotiations

DE   FR

A multinational company in the field of cosmetics is established in more than one hundred countries. The negotiators representing this company in Germany and France are chosen on the basis of the following criteria.

The German culture is rather dogmatic. The observance of rules and even more of dogmas can sometimes take precedence over the search for practical solutions applied to a specific context. The German culture is indeed characterised by a high respect for rules and the search for consensus. Actions causing a breach of the peace are rather badly received. Each individual has the responsibility to respect the established order. It should be noted, however, that the Germans have nonetheless a certain degree of freedom of movement which gives them many individual liberties. If their duties towards society are fulfilled, the Germans can give free rein to their individual preferences. Therefore, when choosing negotiators, you must take this feature into account.

In contrast, in France, the relation to rules is more flexible. Above all, the French put emphasis on the search for solutions adapted to specific contexts and enabling them to take up specific challenges.

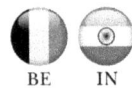
BE IN

In terms of relation to nature, the Belgians have a "do-er" attitude. The "do-er" attitude advocates control over nature. Human activity is of great importance as one assumes to be able to control the environment, which is even desirable. The Belgian negotiator must reflect, through his actions and words, this approach. On the other hand, in terms of relation to nature, the Indians have a "be-er" attitude. The "be-er" attitude advocates adaptation to nature. Great importance is also given to human actions. Nevertheless, in this case, the mission is very different. In India, successes or failures are often considered to be the result of factors external to the environment.

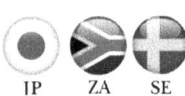
JP ZA SE

Japan and Saudi Arabia are countries with great hierarchical distance. Choosing a senior negotiator can prove an efficient strategy. In contrast, Sweden is a country with low hierarchical distance. Overall, this type of strategy has less impact.

TH

In the Thai society, each individual has a specific role and it is everyone's duty to carefully fulfil his/her role. Failing to do so has an impact on the individual's dignity. In other words, s/he loses face. The notion of status is very important. The social position of people is the result of their Karma and not of their personal achievements. In this perspective, it is recommended to choose somebody considered as having a good karma.

BE

In Belgium, three major political and social trends are important: are you of catholic, social or liberal? The notion of linguistic community is also relevant. The chosen negotiator must be acquainted with these elements and make sure not to blunder.

Importance of table manners in France and Spain and required knowledge for negotiators

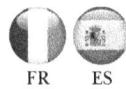

In France, just like in Spain, there is a "table culture". It is recommended to have minimum knowledge of gastronomy and oenology. It is also recommended to take your negotiating partners to good restaurants.

Importance of clothing in the United Kingdom

In the business environment, the choice of clothes is rather conservative, for men as well as for women. It is essential that clothes be of excellent quality. However, they do not necessarily have to be new, unlike in Italy.

The "Bella Figura" concept

For the Italians, the concept of "bella figura" is important. It is a living concept that goes beyond mere appearances. This concept is expressed in several aspects of life, such as:

- behaviour (Overall, the Italians behave in a formal and "sophisticated" manner; this is at least a general trend);
- activities (the Italians appreciate the most sophisticated aspects of life such as art, music, history, quality food, fashion...);
- relations (the Italians like to collaborate with well educated people who have accomplished many things in their lives);
- fashion (in business, elegant and stylish quality clothes are a success factor. Of course, clothes only represent a part of your image).

The chosen negotiator must represent this concept.

Importance of knowing the other parties' cultural heritage

AT   SE

Austria's cultural wealth, stemming from the Austro-Hungarian Empire, is tremendous. The Austrians expect from foreigners to know and value these cultural achievements. In the same way, the Swedish are usually very proud of their regions. Make sure you do not mix them up.

Choice of negotiators

DE   US

In Germany, the level of tolerance to uncertainty is relatively low. Rules and laws shape the perception of the world and decrease the level of uncertainty. Stability and discipline are particularly valued and deviant behaviours are not much tolerated. It is therefore important to choose people who will take this element into account. People able to find solutions while referring to rules in force, people able to provide very concrete and measurable arguments… In contrast, in the United States, the level of tolerance to uncertainty is relatively high. Therefore, your choice should be on people able to take measured risks.

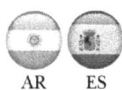
AR   ES

Argentina and Spain have cultures of rather inductive nature. Specific situations and cases are the starting point of many thoughts. General models and theories are based on intuitions. It is important that chosen negotiators be perceived as very pragmatic people and not as theorists.

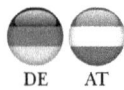
DE   AT

Germany and Austria have cultures of rather deductive nature. Emphasis is laid on theories and general principles. It is from these concepts and logical reasonings that practical applications and solutions arise. It is important to choose negotiators who are very good with concepts.

Notion of network in France

FR

In France, the notion of network is essential. People tend to build networks on the long-term. This trend is reflected in communication modes. Before an important meeting, the French will usually inform their contacts about the sensible points on the agenda. They are informed by their network before, during and after the meeting, as their networks are very active. Being able to develop a quality network is a selection criterion for associates.

One key of success in Ukraine

UA

Business success in Ukraine strongly depends on established personal relations. In this respect, social events are very important. During meals there is usually a bottle of water and a bottle of vodka on the table. Most of the time, the other party expects you to drink vodka as well. Most business entertainment with foreigners takes place in restaurants. Consider it an honour if you are invited at a Ukrainian home. The ability to establish relations is also a determining criterion when choosing associates.

Choice of an intermediary in Japan

JP

Resorting to connections and networks is also very important in Japan. Choose an intermediary of equal status to the person(s) s/he will have to negotiate with. It is essential that intermediaries be not part of the companies involved in the business. For a first contact, if you do not have a specific connection, a phone call is a better option than sending a letter or an email. It is recommended to announce bad news through intermediaries. Using a Japanese business lawyer rather than a Western lawyer is usually perceived as a sign of open-mindedness and collaboration.

Identifying the negotiators' objectives, determining the negotiation threshold and finding common ground

Trying to determine the purpose of a negotiation means asking yourself the following question: what do you want to obtain at the end of the negotiation? It is better to talk about objectives in plural form as you rarely have a single objective. Without clear objectives, you are thrown off balance as soon as the other party makes requests.

It is sound to define and prioritise your objectives before the negotiation. You must distinguish the main objectives from the secondary ones by asking the right questions: what is very important to me? If I have another look at this negotiation one year later, what will indicate me it was a success?

Definition of the objectives

A good objective is always "SMAC":
- Specific: the objective must be formulated in an accurate and detailed way;
- Measurable: you do not necessarily have to put a figure to the objective, but you must be able to see clearly whether it has been achieved or not.
- Accessible: the objective must be realistic;
- Compatible: the objective must be in line with the rest of your objectives.

Classification of the objectives

The objectives may be classified into three distinctive categories:
- ideal objectives (group 1);
- realistic objectives (group 2);
- minimum basic objectives (group 3).

Unrealistic objectives must be put aside at the very beginning. You should assess each objective and determine your priorities.

There are different ways to assess the importance and urgent character of objectives. For example: assign to each objective a value from 0 to 10 reflecting their level of importance and/or urgency. Formulating a sentence to describe each objective makes them more tangible.

Table 4.2. Example of objective assessment

Representatives from several departments gather to discuss an advertising campaign for a "cash cow" product. Each department has its point of view, constraints and objectives. It is nonetheless necessary to act in the best interest of the company and its customers. In order to facilitate the meeting, the members of the communication department gather and formalise their common objectives as a team.		
Objective	**Description of the objective**	**Assessment of the objective**
Win back customers taken away by the competition	Win back 50% of customers > 2000 euros/year taken away by the competition	4
Keep current customers	Increase the level of customers retention by 20%	5
Stimulate trials	Generate 10 000 new trials/year	7
Support sales and increase shares	Increase turnover by 20% and European shares by more than 10%	8

The negotiation threshold

Once your objectives have been clarified and prioritised, you have to define the boundaries of the negotiation, i.e. the points beyond which you refuse to go. This is the negotiation threshold.

According to the case, the negotiation threshold is more or less difficult to determine. The notion of negotiation boundaries or threshold is directly connected to the fallback option concept. The negotiation threshold must be determined according to the cost of the fallback option.

The negotiation threshold must not become an intangible point. Experience shows that a negotiation threshold defined once and for all is a handicap to the negotiation. You must keep room for manoeuvre. In some cases, it is better to set negotiation thresholds corresponding to different levels of concessions you can get from the other party. For example, in a commercial framework, you could set the level of discounts according to the other party's level of orders. Generally speaking, negotiation demands a lot of listening, creativity and agility. This can't be done if the negotiation threshold is too strict.

Finding common ground

A negotiation is like an equation. You must take several parts into consideration. You have to determine everyone's objectives and needs (including yours). We all have our own incentives. Not taking the other party's needs into account is one of the main reasons of failure in negotiation. Focus only on your own needs means you only consider half of the equation and elude a fundamental human factor: "Each individual acts for reasons of his own... not for our reasons."

Make sure to distinguish individual needs from organisational needs, as well as expressed needs from hidden needs.

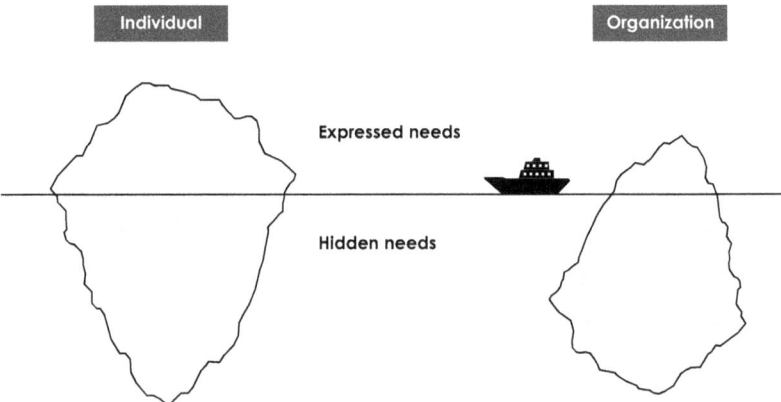

Figure 4.1 – Using the iceberg theory to distinguish individual from organisational needs

Experienced negotiators start with building a common ground. In order to do that, you first have to focus on the other party's needs and determine in what way they coincide with yours.

The cornerstone of common ground is often to be found in the parties' future objectives or in the negotiation process itself. Once the common ground has been identified, you must keep developing and trying to broaden it. The common ground must be an inspiration source for all parties. Working on this common ground leads the parties to find solutions they would probably never have found by focusing only on their own needs.

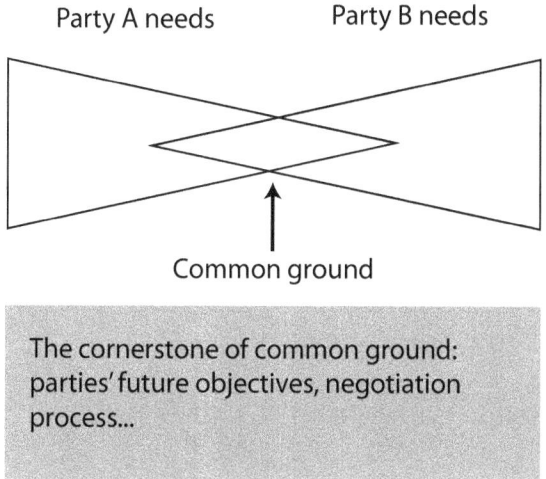

Figure 4.2 – Common ground

- **Classification of needs**

Needs can be classified in different ways. Let us consider the model put forward by Maslow in his book Motivation and Personality. Maslow puts forward five categories of human needs classified according to a determined hierarchy. He suggests that once a level of need is reached, individuals should try to reach the upper level. However, note that this hierarchy can vary from one person to the other, from one cultural group to the other...

- **Example of Maslow's theory application**

Let us imagine somebody is worried about his financial situation. According to Maslow, it would be vain, or even counter-productive, to try and satisfy your needs for self-accomplishment while your needs of security are far from being satisfied. It is only if the situation develops and the person feels more secure that this strategy could bring about positive effects. According to Maslow, the most efficient strategies are those taking into account the needs scale. In negotiation, it is essential to determine the level of the other party's needs.

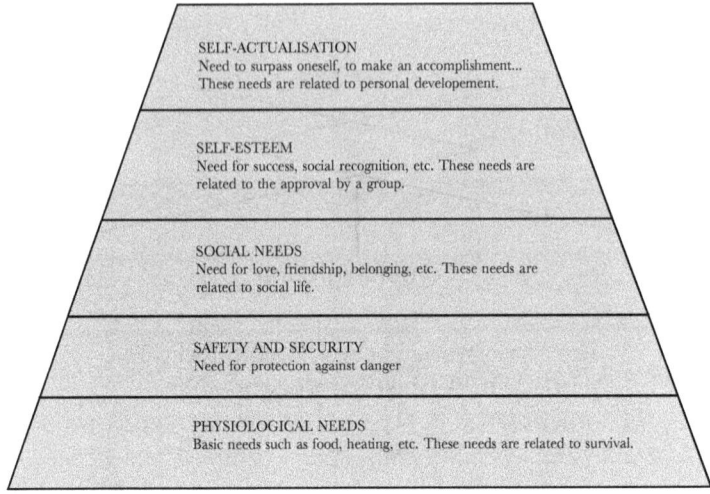

Figure 4.3 – Maslow's pyramid

Case studies

Long-term orientation versus short-term orientation

A long-term oriented nation (like China) shall usually have a clearer outlook for the future than a short-term oriented nation (like South Africa).

Values able to influence the priorities of a negotiation in China

You should know that a great number of Chinese people believe in philosophies like Confucianism. Confucianism has a great influence over the Chinese society. Confucius (Chinese statesman who lived two thousand years ago) established a strict moral and ethical system governing all relations. According to Confucius, family is the basic unit of society and in order to preserve harmony at home you must guarantee the reciprocity of certain relations. Thus, you can observe reciprocal relations between a employer and his employees, a husband and his wife, an elder brother and his younger brother, etc. This Chinese philosophy must be taken into consideration in the negotiation process. In one way or another, the priorities of the negotiation often reflect these values.

Female dominated society versus male dominated society

The Swedish society advocates rather female values (such as well-being, health, balance between family life and professional life...), while the Japanese society, for example, emphasises much more masculine values (such as achievement, duty, material goods...). The objectives pursued by the members of the society are based on these values. For example: pursuit of balance and well-being (in Sweden) or pursuit of financial advantages (in Japan).

Reduction of uncertainty and negotiation priorities

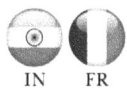

In India, strong social structures leave little room for anxiety. People know and accept their situation in the organisation structure. Behaviours going against religion are not really tolerated. There is a rather strong sense of what Westerners call fatalism. In this perspective, time is not a source of anxiety and the ability to accept things is considered a virtue. In this context, reducing uncertainty is not necessarily a major priority. In contrast, in France, where the level of tolerance to uncertainty is much lower, reducing it can be a major priority. Being appropriately informed is appreciated as it contributes to risk management.

Identifying what influences and motivates parties

CASEPriN is a tool enabling you to easily identify the factors influencing the parties.

Tool: CASEPriN

In negotiation, it is necessary to quickly identify what stimulates action. The "CASEPriN" model gathers these elements in six categories. Paying attention to the vocabulary used by the other party enables you to identify the incentives to action. Words explicitly used often reflect the incentives behind the decisions which implicitly motivate us.

Meaning of CASEPriN:

C = Comfort (people seek simplicity, comfort, quickness)
Key words: simple, easy, functional, fast, convenient...

A = Affection (people seek human contacts, sharing with others)
Key words: the others, us, together, sharing ...

S = Security (people seek firmness, reliability, sustainability)
Key words: strong, reliable, reference, recommended, tested...

E = Economy (people seek efficiency, profitability, savings)
Key words: single chance, last piece, major purchase, economical...

Pri = Pride (people seek exclusiveness, visibility, specialty)
Key words: I, special, gadget, exclusive,...

N = Novelty (people seek novelty, priority)
Key words: novelty, test, pioneering + use of very technical language...

The types of stimuli that influence people depend on their personality, culture and environment in general. Preparing a cultural mapping and analyzing cultural dimensions helps to identify these stimuli.

Case studies

The notions of honour and shame in China

CH

In China, the concept of shame is very important. An individual should not bring disgrace upon himself or his family.

Zhang Shuhong, co-owner of the company Lee Der Industrial, committed suicide when China announced a temporary banning of exports by the company after 967 000 toys were recalled due to the amount of lead in the paint.

Based on popular characters such as "Elmo", "Big Bird" and "Dora and Diego", the toys were produced by Lee Der for Mattel, which trades Fisher-Price in the United States. Zhang's best friend sold the paint to Lee Der.

"The boss and the company were harmed by the paint supplier" said a manager at the company, who added "it is common for disgraced Chinese officials to commit suicide."

"CNN News, August 14th 2007, CEO Commits Suicide Over Fisher-Price Recall."

Tolerance to uncertainty as a factor of influence

FR   BE

The level of tolerance to uncertainty can be an important factor of influence. Belgium and France have a relatively low level of tolerance to uncertainty compared, for example, to Sweden or the Philippines. A low level does not mean that no risks will be taken, but rather that there will be more risk assessment efforts.

DE

In Germany, a lot of participants intervene in the decision-making process. In addition to the official command chain, German organizations usually have a parallel set of consultants and decision-makers. The approval of this "shadow cabinet" is often necessary.

Analyzing the situation

All negotiations imply stakes. Each party holds cards (or resources) and expects winnings. The cards, or trump cards, are power instruments for the parties. The expected benefits determine the negotiation objectives. In order to efficiently negotiate, you have to know as accurately as possible which are the parties' arguments and the benefits they expect.

The actual stakes are not always obvious, which makes things difficult. Most of the times, the negotiators ignore the actual stakes of the discussion for the other parties. Hence, the need to have good information upstream of the negotiation process and pay attention throughout the discussion.

Cost/impact or cost/risk matrix

Let us first consider the resources of each party. The idea is not only to make a list of these advantages, but also to assess the extent to which each party is willing to use their trump cards. In other words: determine how far each party is ready to go.

Indeed, having a specific power does not mean you are willing to use it. Moreover, using certain cards may incur more cost that profit.

▸ **Cost/impact matrix**

The cost/impact matrix is used to assess the position of the negotiating parties, provided you have enough information.

The *cost* corresponds to negative effects induced by the execution of a threat or the granting of a concession. This cost may be low or high. Its value may be roughly assessed or, alternatively, clearly quantified.

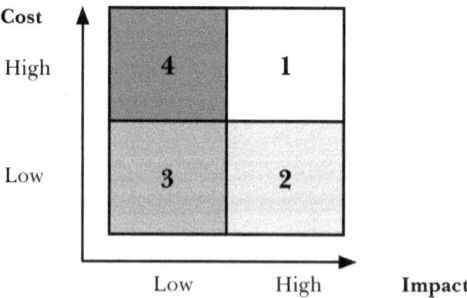

Figure 4.4 – The cost/impact matrix

The *impact* defines the importance of a potential risk caused by a threat, or the potential value of a concession.

The junction of impact and cost creates four areas on the matrix. You must place all your trump cards in these four boxes.

1st Area: Compromise. High impact and cost. These cards must be used carefully and more specifically in case of tensions.

2nd Area: Strength. The impact is high and the cost is low. This card can be used at the beginning of the negotiation. Of course, it doesn't mean you have to carry out all your "threats". It is only an option.

3rd Area: "Small benefits". Low impact and cost. These cards can be used from time to time to demonstrate your power. It is nonetheless recommended to use them carefully in order not to lose credibility.

4th Area: Waste. The impact is lower and the cost is high. The use these cards often results in weakening the position of the one who uses them. The other party often realises you are using poor trumps. It is recommended not to use these cards.

How to use the cost/impact matrix?

At first, make a list of all the cards you have. Then, place them in the different areas of the matrix. This is very useful for further proceedings, as it gives a clear view of the arguments you can develop and in which order. The most costly trumps must be the last to be presented.

If while trying to fill in the matrix you realise you have no or few trumps in boxes 1 and 2, you should find new ones quickly, otherwise the negotiation is going to be difficult. This may mean finding more information about the other party or even preparing a sound fallback option.

Then, do the same by putting yourself in the other party's shoes. This second analysis will be called "cost/risk" matrix. Under these circumstances, the risk is equivalent to the one you are running. Put yourself in the other party's position and try to determine what s/he is up to. What advantages – as far as you know – does the other party dispose of? What would be the impact on you if these cards were to be used? By proceeding this way, you will be able to prepare yourself more efficiently and to anticipate future reactions or "retaliation".

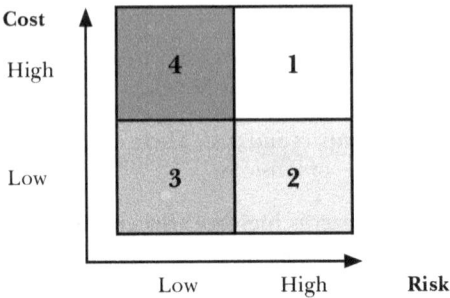

Figure 4.5 – The cost/risk matrix

Example of cards or trumps classification

Airfly is an aircraft manufacturer, with a turnover of 10 billions in 2010. One of the main directions of its strategy is to improve their aircrafts' efficiency in order to make them cheaper, safer and, above all, more ecological.

Airfly managers have decided to give a first try to the G212, a relatively small plane used for short distance flights.

LiegeCo is a Belgian SME of 50 employees specialised in the optimisation of aeronautical engines. A patent on a really innovative optimisation tool was licensed this year. LiegeCo was even awarded a prize for this breakthrough.

Today, Airfly represents 30% of LiegeCo's turnover. These two companies have been collaborating for more than ten years.

Airfly is willing to sign an exclusive contract with LiegeCo for the improvement of the G212 engine.

In this example, Goliath needs David, and vice versa.

Proposal of classification of Airfly's trump cards at this stage:
- 1st Area (compromise): Draw back from the business. This option is very risky. LiegeCo needs a strong partner in order to develop and commercialise its prototypes. Airfly needs to distinguish itself in a more and more competitive environment;
- 2nd Area (strength): Play on volumes. If the test is conclusive, the partnership could be extended to several models of aircrafts;
- 3rd Area (small benefits): Include, in a draft agreement, a strong

penalty for LiegeCo in case the prototype is not ready on time (if the deadline is too short). This strategy of pressure could have negative effects in some partnerships;
- 4th Area (waste): Include, in a draft agreement, an exclusion clause for LiegeCo in case the prototype would not be ready on time. Rejecting a partner will not help Airfly to become more competitive on its market.

Advice: bear prices and values in mind. If you have to enter a negotiation in which the financial aspect plays a significant part, it is recommended to lay emphasis on the value of your concessions or on the consequences of your threats. This does not necessarily mean you should hold up this assessment from the outset. You should only go ahead with it if the other party does not seem to realise the value of what you offer, or the consequences of the threat hanging over them.

Stakes analysis matrix

In order to make the analysis easier, let us consider that the parties involved in the negotiation – i.e. the stakeholders – are acting in a generally reasonable manner and try to achieve objectives by using their trump cards and taking their constraints into account.

The stakes analysis enables you to anticipate the stakeholders' potential behaviour and, at a later stage, to carry on the negotiation accordingly.

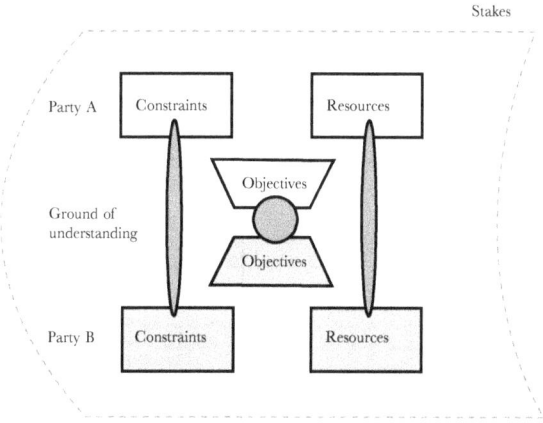

Figure 4.6 – Stakes analysis matrix

For each stakeholder, the following elements should be included in the analysis:
- the potential objectives (announced objectives versus hidden objectives);
- the key motives (it is recommended to provide the factual explanation concerning the reason for which you note down a specific motive rather than another);
- the actual request (beyond the apparent request, which is the stakeholders' actual request?) ;
- the resources;
- the constraints;
- your common groundwith the stakeholder;
- the possible strategy;
- the impact on you (consider the impact – be it positive or negative – that the stakeholder has on your objective. In what way does s/he threaten to slow you down or, alternatively, how can s/he provide support to you?)

Stakeholders	Possible objectives	Key motives	Actual request	Resources	Constraints	Common ground	Possible strategy	Impact on you

Using this table and the list of your power levers, among others things, will help you clarify your negotiation strategy.

In the case of a "simple" strategy involving a limited number of parties, you could consider a simplified version of the stakeholders matrix.

Stakeholders	Possible objectives	Resources	Constraints	Common ground	Possible strategy	Impact on you

Example of analysis of the stakeholders' objectives, resources and constraints: sale of a second hand car

Al Dar is a North Africa based company selling second hand family cars. One of the two founders, Mister Saïd, wishes to diversify the company's activity by selling luxury saloon cars. Mister Nouri, his associate, is not against the idea, but wishes to stick to the planned budget for the September supplies.

Mister Saïd and Mister Nouri have been associates for more than twenty years. They own 80% and 20% respectively of the company's shares. Note that Mister Nouri is more involved in the daily management of the company.

Imagine you are the Belgian seller and that the price you ask for your of family cars and top range saloon cars lot is slightly higher than what the buyers had expected.

You are then in position to negotiate.

Question 1. Which objectives should you influence and how?

In this case, Mr. Nouri and Mr. Saïd's objectives are partially different. What does Mr. Nouri exactly mean by "sticking to the planned budget"?

Which information ruled over this budget's definition? Is it a long-term perspective? If so, can you lay emphasis on the car's value on the North African market and on the fact it will last longer? On the other hand, if it is a short-term perspective, you can lay emphasis on payment terms. After the discussion, it turns out to be the second case.

Question 2. Which resources can you exploit?

There are different ways of acting on resources. Presenting several newspaper cuttings displaying similar offers at a higher cost is a way of acting on one of the other party's resources: the call for competition.

This is only one option amongst many others.

Question 3. Which constraints can you modify?

In this case, time has to be on your side. This element can be used as a lever.

Question 4. What is the common ground?

If you are in no hurry to receive the full payment for your car lot, the terms of settlement could represent a good cornerstone for the common ground. A second cornerstone could be the good communication between the parties. These points are only a few examples of those which can be underlined.

Table 4.3. Example of analysis of the stakeholders' objectives, resources and constraints

Stakeholders	Objectives	Resources	Constraints	Common ground	Likely strategy(ies)
Mr. Nouri	Purchasing a reliable car lot while sticking to the planned budget	Power of influence on his colleague	Having the car lot on time. Do not quarrel with his colleague	Settlement periods. Interactions between buyers and sellers	Finding other offers if necessary. Putting forward the observance of the budget to his colleague
Mr. Saïd	Buying a family and luxury saloon car lot	Control over the final decision	Having the car lot on time. Do not quarrel with his colleague		Ask the seller for a discount. Convince his colleague
Belgian seller	Selling his car lot at the expected price, or even more	Other potential buyers	Selling the car lot before the end of the month		Play with time and competition

This analysis grid can be very efficient if you have made some enquiries about the other party or if you know the elements in question. You can always try to anticipate them.

Case studies

Identifying the sources of information in order to perform a good analysis of the situation

TN   MA   US   UK

In high context societies (e.g. Tunisia or Morocco), information circulates through networks and must be interpreted in its context. Formal information usually represents only a small part. In contrast, in low context societies (like the United States or the United Kingdom), much more formal information is usually available on paper.

Once you know what you are looking for, you have to know where to look!

Analyzing the way of introducing oneself as a good source of information for stakeholder identification

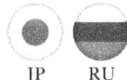

JP   RU

Japanese is a rich language which includes many ways of addressing somebody. The choice is made according to such criteria as title, age, level of responsibilities… Therefore, do not be surprised if your Japanese interlocutors ask many questions to their visitors. They need this information in order to know how to best address them.

In Russia, first and last names are listed in the same way as in Western countries. Nevertheless, you should know that the second Christian name is often patronymic, i.e. a name derived from the father's name. For example: Marat Safin means Marat, son of Safin. Russian women usually add the letter "a" at the end of their last name. Medvedev's wife becomes Mrs. Medvedeva. The Russians use lots of nicknames and diminutives between them. If they ask you to call them in such way, it is a proof of friendship and proximity.

Knowing who you are dealing with is essential in negotiation!

Impact of the notion of authority on data analysis

ID

The Indonesians have much respect for authority. In that way, the boss will often be told what he wants to hear, but this does not mean he is being told the truth. The truth is often communicated privately, by a friend. A foreign executive needs to establish a network through which he will have access to the truth. One of the way Indonesians prove their respect for their bosses is to prevent them from hearing bad news in public. The leitmotiv "Make papa happy" is instilled in Indonesian children from very early age. The saying "Silence is consent" is not universally valid. It is essential to take these elements into account when gathering data.

In short, knowing where to look for information is not enough, you still have to know the way to get it and analyze the results with careful consideration.

Choosing a negotiating style, identifying the other parties' style and choosing a negotiation strategy

Negotiators have a complete set of behaviours to display. Identifying the extent to which these behaviours are competitive or collaborative is an excellent way of classifying them.

First, you should know that, **in absolute terms, there are no good or bad styles.** Experienced negotiators knowingly choose their negotiating style according to the circumstances and the expected results. Any style can turn out to be counter-productive, if it is not adapted to the situation.

All negotiators have their favourite style. Nevertheless, the ability to consciously adapt your negotiating style is a key factor of success. It is recommended to identify your favourite negotiating style as well as the ones of your partners and interlocutors.

Classification of negotiating styles

Behaviours can be represented along a scale, ranging from very competitive (dark grey) to very collaborative (light grey).

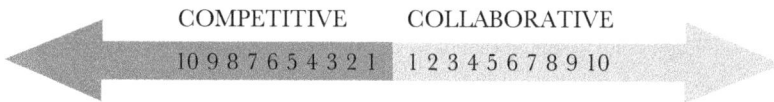

Figure 4.7 – Scale representing the negotiating style

On one edge of the scale, competitive negotiators are considered as dominant, aggressive and authoritarian. On the other edge of the scale, collaborative negotiators may seem accommodating, some times even going as far as acting against their own interests. Closer from the centre are the supportive or even assertive negotiators who do not lapse into excess or caricature.

Table 4.4. Characteristics of negotiators

Characteristics of competitive negotiators	Characteristics of collaborative negotiators
Competitive negotiators are more inclined to…	*Collaborative negotiators are more inclined to…*
try and dominate the other party	interact with the other negotiators on equal terms
consider the other negotiators as opponents	consider the other negotiators as partners rather than opponents
start the negotiation on a tough line, often with unreasonable requests	start the negotiation with reasonable and realistic requests
be hardly flexible	be flexible
plan emotional reactions	be rational (few premeditated use of emotions)
ask important concessions while granting few	make mutual concessions

Characteristics of competitive negotiators	Characteristics of collaborative negotiators
be evasive, withhold information and bluff	share information and be open
Make assertions rather than ask questions (one-way communication)	ask questions rather than make assertions (real communication in both ways)
use force, power, even threat to win people to their cause	use compromise rather than force
Display preconceived ideas from the start	seek win-win solutions (solutions meeting the expectations of all parties)
show no or little interest in the other party's needs and feelings and focus on short-term and benefits for your own side	show interest for the other party's needs and feelings
think in win-lose terms and consider a lose-lose situation in case the other party could not be defeated	think in win-win terms

Choice of a negotiating style

The choice depends on the context and particularly on the expected results on the short and long-term. The choice of style can also be influenced by other factors such as the perception of the other party's level of implication, the duration of the relation, the nature of the benefit... Nevertheless, it is the final result and not the context which must be the determining factor of influence. Anticipating the impact of the choice of style on the whole situation remains important.

It is perfectly possible to vary style and to be, for example, rather collaborative in terms of process and more competitive in terms of content. In negotiation, it is essential to always draw a distinction between content and process (or form) (figure 4.8).

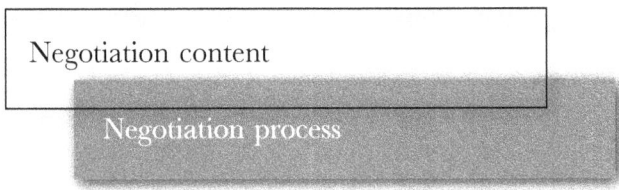

Figure 4.8 – Distinction between content and process (or form) of negotiation

Several points must be considered when developing a strategy:
- how to develop and choose your strategy?
- how many people will be part of the negotiation team?
- how long will it take to develop your strategy?
- should the whole team participate in the negotiation?
- should you envisage practising before starting the negotiation?
- …

In the scope of the stakes matrix (figure 4.9), three types of possible actions must be considered:
1. Influencing the other party's objectives;
2. Modifying the resources of some stakeholders;
3. Modifying the constraints of some stakeholders.

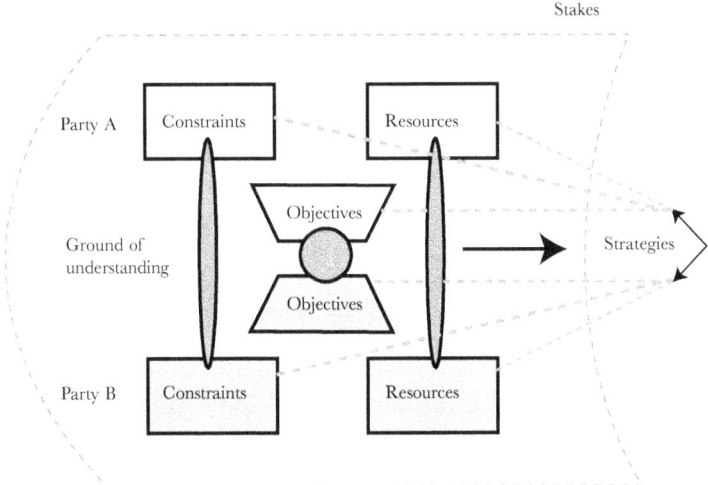

Figure 4.9 – Development of a strategy based on the stakes analysis matrix

At this stage, it is wise to complete the stakes matrix by indicating the actions to undertake vis-à-vis the stakeholders.

Stakeholders	Possible objectives	Key motives	Actual request	Resources	Constraints	Common ground	Possible strategy	Impact on you	Actions to undertake

Strategic use of trump cards

Choosing your trump cards and deciding to use them (according to their cost/impact ratio) means laying the groundwork. The way you organise these cards is of crucial importance. Generally speaking, it is recommended to abide by the following principles:

- always suggest concessions much smaller than what you are ready to offer (each proposal is considered as a new starting ground);
- plan concessions of decreasing importance, i.e. the impact on the other party and the cost for yourself are decreasing;
- allowing yourself time to think;
- not revealing all your cards.

Showing one of your cards means hinting at a possibility, whereas "playing" your winning card means actually achieving something.

Weiss' model of culturally responsive strategies

There is a vast number of strategies. There are potentially as many strategies as situations. Therefore, the choice shall depend on the situation, the level of knowledge and the culture of the other party, the future prospects, etc. However, there is a relevant and interesting model which is worth presenting: the Weiss' model of culturally responsive strategies . According to Weiss[14], there are culturally responsive strategies (figure 4.10) which apply particularly well to the contexts of international negotiation. These eight strategies are based on the cultural knowledge of negotiators and their ability to efficiently use this knowledge in social interactions.

---

14 Weiss S., "Negotiating with Romans", *Sloan Management Review*, 1994

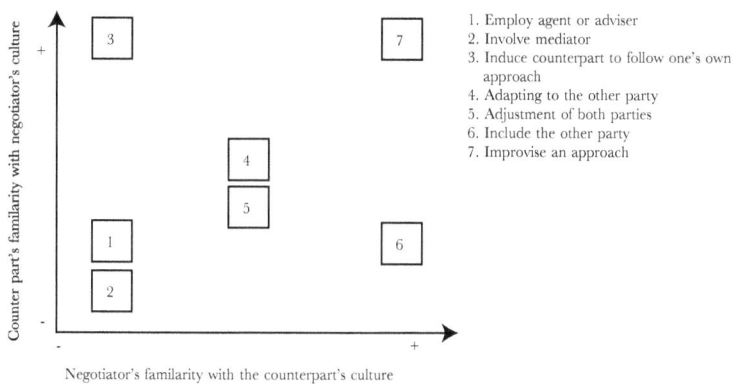

Figure 4.10 – Model of culturally responsive strategies

For each level of familiarity, the negotiator can use strategies corresponding to his own level as well as to all the lower levels.

According to this model, negotiators with limited knowledge of the other party's culture should use one of the starting strategies (1-3). Negotiators with an intermediate knowledge of the other party's culture should focus primarily on the two following levels (4-5). Finally, it is recommended for negotiators with good knowledge of the other party's culture to focus on the two last strategies (6-7).

Strategic choice of the number of negotiators

In a multilateral negotiation, it is essential to assign a role to each member of the group. Five main roles can be distinguished:

Table 4.5. The five main types of negotiators

Role	Responsibility
The leader: all negotiation teams need a leader. The choice of the leader highly depends on culture.	The leader leads the negotiation and invites if necessary and/or possible other people to take part. He manages the team's resources throughout the process. He guides the members of his team.

Role	Responsibility
The good guy: the interlocutors rather identify themselves to this person. Some times, the other party would like this person to be the only contact.	Providing a feeling of safety to the other party. In some cases, this person can give the impression of being in conflict with his own team.
The bad guy: this role often gives the other parties the impression that a compromise is impossible to reach.	He tries to "intimidate" the other team and to lay emphasis on their weaknesses. He challenges the other party's arguments. He slows down the negotiation process.
The unbending: this team member is very rigid on many subjects. He does not attend all negotiation sessions but the other members often make reference to him.	He enables the negotiators to withdraw offers they may have made too quickly. He reminds the team's objectives to the group.
The observer: This person listens to the points of view and arguments of all participants and makes relevant summaries that he then shares with the group.	He puts forward methods or strategies to break the deadlock. This person takes note of all inconsistent arguments.

Case studies

The way of approaching a negotiation differs from one culture to the other. For example:
- in the Middle-East, rather than approaching subjects sequentially, negotiators often choose to discuss several problems at the same time;
- in South America, negotiators can adopt a very physically animated negotiation style;
- in Japan, negotiators usually work as a team and the search for consensus prevails during the decision making process;
- in China, negotiators are trained in the art of winning concessions;
- in Germany, decisions can take much longer.

This fact is, amongst other things, connected to the need to analyze information in depth and to call upon experts.

Development of a push strategy aiming at penetrating the Egyptian market of medical equipment.

EG   US

An American company of medical equipment targets the Egyptian market. The sales team, supported by a marketing and communication team, develops an exceptional market penetration strategy. It is mid-December, and the objective is to finalise 80% of the sales by the end of the month. For this purpose, a rather active, even aggressive strategy has been elaborated. The communication manager of the project raises a point. Doing business in Egypt needs patience. Delays are part of everyday life. The following words, very common in Egypt, reflect this fact:

- *Bokra*, which means "tomorrow";
- *Inscha'allah*, which means "God willing";
- *Malesh*, which means "never mind".

The negotiation rhythm is much slower in Egypt than it usually is in Western countries. The Egyptians follow their own rhythm. Trying to make them take decisions more quickly than they wish would probably be useless and certainly counter-productive. This element must be taken into account when developing strategies.

Risk taking and developing strategies

RO   BE

Every strategy includes some risk. It is essential to know how this risk is perceived in order to integrate it harmoniously in your strategy. For example, in Romania, boldness is much valued. The Romanians are usually unpredictable, spontaneous and able to take risks. In contrast, in Belgium risks are rather calculated. However, this does not prevent many innovative projects to see the light of day.

Strategy development in Sweden

SE

The four following concepts are of fundamental importance in the Swedish culture: egalitarianism, neutrality, well-being and respect of human life and nature:
- egalitarianism: even if authority is respected, having a high-ranking position does not necessarily offer specific privileges. Many Swedes believe that hierarchy can be circumvented if necessary;
- neutrality: this concept has been reflected in the country's foreign policy for decades. Despite their neutral status, the Swedish consider they are free to give their opinions on surrounding injustices and problems;
- well-being: do not rush a Swede that is getting a break;
- respect of human life and nature: priority is given to the quality of life and the environment.

Company policies in Sweden usually reflect these values. You could also use these principles when developing your strategies.

Choice of a strategy in the United States

US

The United States definitely advocate control over nature rather than adaptation to it. This feature is an integral part of the American culture and is reflected in the strategies adopted by its members. The adopted strategies must be of "interventionist" nature. Chance plays a very limited part in such an environment where man controls nature.

Choice between a change-oriented strategy and a stability-oriented strategy

US BE

The United States are a change-oriented nation. It is through change that this "young" nation was created again and again. In contrast, the Belgian society is rather stability-oriented; this does not prevent it though from developing and leaving room for change. These are basic general trends which you have to take into account when developing strategies.

Choice between a competition-oriented strategy and a collaboration-oriented strategy

IP UK

In the United Kingdom, competition is rather important, even in the education system. In contrast, in Japan, the notion of collaboration is given more value and goes hand in hand with the search for long-term solutions.

Connection between the level of tolerance to uncertainty and the choice of a negotiation strategy

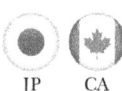

IP CA

In Japan, the level of tolerance to uncertainty is relatively low. From the earliest age the Japanese learn that it conformity and avoidance of embarrassing situations are necessary. Sound professional ethics and strong group relations bring stability to life. The chosen negotiation strategies usually imply reasonable risk taking.

In contrast, in Canada, the chosen negotiation strategies can be more risky. The Canadians have a rather high tolerance to uncertainty. Several elements can provide stability: external structures are social structures, an objective approach to the world...

Impact of the approach type (analytical or systemic) when choosing a strategy

EG IP

The Egyptian and Japanese cultures are of rather systemic nature. More attention is given to the whole than to the components. Each issue or subject is considered as a whole and emphasis is laid on the link that might exist between the different components. The adopted strategies must be considered from a systemic point of view and not in a segmented manner.

Organising the meeting and interactions

This subject was already touched upon in "climate management". Nevertheless, its relevance can never be emphasised enough! Efficiently organising the meeting is a key factor of success in negotiation as well as an integral part of a good preparation.

Identifying practices in terms of protocol and communication

This subject shall be further developed in the following chapters. By referring to the iceberg theory, you realise that "the visible world" (behaviours, language, etc.) is not perceived in the same way by everyone. We all have a set of guidelines through which we analyze the course of events. Moreover, what is desirable in one culture is not necessarily desirable in another. There are more misunderstandings than disagreements. It is essential to be informed beforehand about local habits and customs in terms of protocol and communication. For this reason, you should identify the current codes in terms of greetings, use of titles and forms, gesture codes, offering of gifts, dress code, etc.

Identifying entertainment habits

What is the place of entertainment in the business environment? Is entertainment an integral part of the business world or is it considered an option?

What does entertainment mean? This notion does not have the same meaning for everyone and what is considered as appropriate in one culture is not necessarily considered the same way in another one.

What is the purpose of entertainment? Is it to briefly get to know one another or to "tame" each other?

What does an invitation to entertainment mean? Is it an honour or, on the contrary, commonplace?

It is recommended to get acquainted beforehand with the habits and customs in terms of entertainment. This makes the negotiation process run smooth.

Example: entertainment habits in Australia

AU

You should know that in Australia, it is common for everyone to buy a round. If you don't, you will definitely give a false impression of yourself. If you are invited for a drink, seize the opportunity to establish good relations with the other party instead of talking business. Note that it is unusual for Australians to invite strangers immediately to their homes. They first take the time to get to know you. Being invited into an Australian home is considered a honour. These points must be taken into consideration when preparing a negotiation.

▸ **Organising the meeting**

It is recommended to pay particular attention to the agenda and to the venue. These elements are not simple details, but they can strongly influence the course of the negotiation.

• *Using the agenda as a negotiation tool*

It is recommended to include a list of topics for discussion in the draft agenda. This enables the parties to agree beforehand on the topics which will be addressed and those which will be intentionally discarded. The time allotted for each topic must be reasonable. Each participant must get a copy of the agenda.

In some cases, the agenda can be negotiated. If possible, it is recommended to limit to two hours the duration of each session. It is also recommended to put clocks in sight in order to guarantee that participants realise that time goes by.

Example: the meaning of being late

In countries like Japan or China, punctuality is of crucial importance. Being late can be considered as insulting. In contrast, in Southern Europe, being late for a meeting is not as important as in China.

• *Using the meeting venue and atmosphere as a negotiation tool*

The outcome of a negotiation strongly depends on the atmosphere. The venue is one of the elements influencing this atmosphere.

Intercultural Negotiation

The way negotiators are seated can have an impact on the course of the debate and, therefore, the final result (table 4.6). Except for negotiations of a specific nature, it is recommended to negotiate in teams of maximum five people. Note that the participants must have the possibility to contact, if necessary, people from outside the negotiation group.

Table 4.6 – Choice of the negotiators' seats

Venue	Elements to consider
Small group	People are often facing each other. A round table may prove more suitable than a square table.
Big group	Participants are placed around a podium or a table.

Potential layout of seats:

1　2　3　4　5

Your team - The other party

6　6　3　6　6

1　The bad guy
2　The good guy
3　The leader
4　The unbending
5　The observer
6　Unknown role

- It is often recommended to seat the "bad guy" on the edge of the table, away from the group.
- The "good guy" is often seated beside the leader, in order to strengthen positive feelings towards your group.
- The leader is usually seated in the centre of the group because he must be able to easily get in contact with all participants.
- The observer is seated where he has a good visibility on the other party's team.

Once these points have been addressed, you can proceed to the next stage: the conduct of the negotiation.

Case studies

Attempt to organise a meeting during Chinese New Year

CH US

A brand manager from an American company selling sportswear tries to organise a meeting with a subsidiary in China. Sales have markedly decreased to the benefit of a local brand and the brand manager wishes to clarify the situation as soon as possible. He suggests three dates during the same week and is surprised that none is suitable.

An associate points out that it is Chinese New Year's time. This celebration, still called the Spring Festival, is one of the most important yearly celebrations in China. According to the tradition, every Chinese should return to his birthplace at this time. This leads millions of Chinese to travel in a very short period of time. So, it is not recommended to travel at this time of the year.

The Chinese go by the lunar calendar while a majority of people coming from Western countries go by the solar calendar.

Attempt to organise a meeting during Ramadan

ID

With more than 240 million inhabitants, Indonesia is the country with the biggest Muslim population in the world. While Islam is not the official religion, Indonesia has been declared a monotheistic nation, which goes in hand with Islam and is opposed to Hinduism. The Indonesians adapted Islam to their needs.

Ramadan is an Islamic tradition of fundamental importance. During this important period of time, business slows down. Ramadan starts with the new moon on the first night of the Chaabane month. The Muslim calendar is based on lunar cycles.

Organisation of a first contact in China and in Turkey

CH   TR

In Turkey, like in China, the elders are treated with respect. It may be interesting to call upon older or more experienced people to establish a first contact or, at least, to use their presence as a "guarantee indicator".

Organisation of a business trip in China by a French cosmetics manager

CH   FR

The parent company asks the French cosmetics manager to visit a subsidiary in China in order to sort out some points linked to a current project. In the aim of making the most of her journey, she makes a list of points to discuss and of people to meet. Before leaving, she sends the full planning to her Chinese interlocutor and thanks him in advance for organising the necessary meetings.

Once in Shanghai, holding in her hands a copy of the unreplied email she sent, the manager tries immediately to take stock of the situation with her interlocutor. A bit confused by this approach, he confirms that she is expected by the whole team, that many decisions have to be taken and that she can take the seat specifically reserved for her. A few minutes later, the manager comes back to him with her list of points to discuss. His reaction is to grab his phone and, after several conversations in Chinese, inform her that her first interlocutor is coming to see her.

At this point, she is disappointed and thinks her stay will be utterly unproductive and a waste of time, as it appears impossible to efficiently plan her time under these conditions.

However, the next developments are going to reassure her. All the parties of the project come to see her and all the subjects are gradually discussed, while the way things are coordinated is rather unclear. At the end of the week, all the points on her list have been discussed and dealt with.

What's bred in the bone comes out in the flesh... For her second mission, the manager has a new list of tasks. It is hard for her to understand that her Chinese colleagues have a different approach to time. They don't quite understand her wish to exploit every single minute of her time. She doesn't quite understand either how time can be considered a daily routine or how things can be sometimes left for the following day.

For her third journey, the manager arrives in Shangai without "disturbing" anyone with her plans and lists of tasks. Now that she has integrated the local pace, she takes pleasure watching the development of actions and taking decisions gradually, without the stress related to the planning of overlapping meetings. She then realises that appointments are not arranged in the same way in China and in France. An appointment arranged "long" in advance may not take place. It is only when discussing a topic involving a provider that you contact him and he often arrives within a few hours in order to participate to the discussion and, when an internal topic has to be discussed, comes out and waits for one hour in the reception area. To the French manager's great surprise, the provider does not seem offended by this method and, in principle, no one considers he is wasting his time.

Before a visit of her Chinese interlocutor to France, the latter confirms on Wednesday that he will be arriving on Sunday in Paris, whereas she tends to plan her business trips at least four weeks in advance.

In conclusion, the Chinese and French methods are both effective and, despite the fact that the Chinese hardly plan their meetings, business is handled at the same pace, even sometimes more quickly. The Chinese consider that time is circular; it repeats itself and it is therefore useless to hurry. In contrast, Westerners consider that time is linear; it ticks by and never repeats itself.

Organisation of a meeting with representatives from Argentina

AR

The Argentinians have the reputation of being serious. Being serious is an essential feature for doing business in Argentina. All aspects of the meeting's organisation (elaboration and communication of the agenda, choice of the venue, etc.) must reflect this fact. The material communicated must be of good quality. Details are highly importance.

Choice of the number of negotiators and of the venue

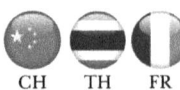
CH TH FR

China and Thailand have cultures of rather collectivist nature. It is rare to send a single negotiator on mission and more common to form an entire delegation. In contrast, it is common in France, which is a rather individualistic country, to send a single negotiator. Reception facilities and the number of representatives must be adapted to the cultural specificities.

Organisation of a negotiation meeting between partners from Russia, Romania, Saudi Arabia and Ukraine

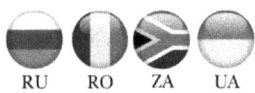
RU RO ZA UA

These cultures value prestige. It is strongly recommended to organise the meeting in a prestigious location.

Booking hotel rooms for the participants

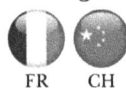
FR CH

What a surprise for a Frenchman to see three or four of his Chinese colleagues, on a business trip to France, staying in the small apartment of a fellow Chinese man living in France for a few months. The first conclusion, linked to the French perception of space, is to consider these people are saving money, or even that they don't have enough money to stay at the hotel. In fact, while "living together" is considered a source of embarrassment in France, it is not the case in China. Chinese children are used to see two or three generations living under the same roof: their grandparents, their parents and themselves. This is a common situation and the supreme happiness is having "four generations under a same roof". Even nowadays, these children seldom have their own room. They sleep in their parents' bedroom, or even in their bed. A young Chinese seldom leaves his parents' home before getting married, unless he has to study away from home. Therefore, the notion of personal space is perceived very differently by Chinese and French adults. Within French families, the child quickly learns the notion of individual space. In the middle and upper classes of the French society, the goal of families is often to have one room for each child. When studying away from home, these young people often have their own room, or share it with a fellow student. Later, for business trips, single rooms are not necessarily booked for each person.

Financial audit of a French company bought out by a Chinese group

FR   CH

A French company is bought out by a Chinese company. The finance department of the Chinese company makes a routine audit of its new subsidiary and realises that travelling expenses are dangerously increasing due to the increasing number of projects between France and China and the numerous trips required. Despite an express request from the Chinese company to better manage travelling expenses, these are still very high on the French side in comparison with their Chinese counterparts. Consequently, the Chinese finance department puts forward more restrictive economic rules and significantly reduces the French budget. As the French do not share their space naturally, (in this case hotel rooms, apartments, etc.) they decrease the number of business trips inn order to stick to their budgets. However, the Chinese culture is based on oral communication. Therefore, this decision has a direct impact on the smooth running of projects.

Space structuring and choice of the negotiation venue in France, in China, in Germany, in Sweden and in the United States

FR   TR   DE   SE   US

According to sociologists, the office is part of the so-called "primary" territories, along with accommodation, cars in developed countries, etc. They also say that the working space has a dual role: practical and symbolic. In this case, symbolic means that it gives an indication on his occupant's status and that it has a social meaning.

In France, like in China, in Germany and in the United States, the working space is a power indicator. For example, managers often have their own offices, heads of departments a partitioned space and engineers share an open space, semi-partitioned or not partitioned, etc.

There is an interesting difference between China and France in the way they deal with this fact. While in France, egalitarianism is officially advocated in speeches (probably a heritage of the French Revolution), in China, differences are openly accepted. However, having your own office in China seems to be even more important than in France. Let us take the example of an engineer being asked by his new French Head of Department to leave his office in order to go and work with his colleagues in the open space. He reacts vehemently and makes immediately an appointment with the Human Resources Manager to discuss this issue. This situation is perceived as an unthinkable loss of power. What would be considered in France as a mere reorganisation of the landscape is perceived as an irreversible mistake by the Chinese colleague. After loosing face in front of his peers, he decides to leave the company. Note that this happens in a specific context suitable for turnover. Consequently, the Head of Department probably loses a useful resource for the company.

In the American culture, the hierarchical position is determined by the number of windows you have in your working space. Engineers are often in the centre of the open spaces and managers on the sides. The number and size of windows can be an indicator of the occupant's position in the hierarchy.

In the German culture, space also has a strong meaning. Let us consider the example of a German company having its central offices in a multi-storey building. Offices are allocated by floor according the occupants' position in the hierarchy. The highest floor is exclusively reserved to the company's CEO! There even are canteens accessible only to specific groups.

In the Swedish culture, everyone has an office of relatively equal size and style. The General Manager usually has a barely bigger office than his colleagues.

When choosing the negotiation venue, it is essential to take the value of space into account and choose a place in line with the parties' beliefs and preferences.

Organisation of a social event in Indonesia

ID

Organising a social event or a party can be tricky in Indonesia. It is recommended to send written invitations (addressed to the husband and his wife) at least one week in advance. You should know that many Indonesians are reluctant to make long-term commitments concerning social events and do not necessarily confirm their presence in writing. It is therefore recommended to come up with a good excuse to contact again the guests, over the phone or in person, in order to remind them of the event. Be prepared to answer questions about the event, the guest list and the guest of honour. Parties usually start early as many people leave around 9.30 – 10 p.m. The Indonesians tend to prefer buffets over seated diners with assigned seats. Make sure the food is sophisticated. Don't forget that Muslims do not drink alcohol and that Hindus do not eat beef. Always treat the guest of honour with the utmost respect. S/he is usually the last to arrive and the first to be served.

You should know that being invited to social events is important in Indonesia. You may not be immediately invited. In that case, be patient. It is usually recommended to wait for your Indonesian interlocutor to invite you first.

Organisation of a meeting

RU

When inviting Russians, always make sure there is enough food and drinks. During business meetings, the Russians always make sure there is a variety of drinks and food available and expect the same in return. The notion of abundance is important.

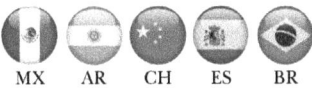
MX   AR   CH   ES   BR

In Mexico, like in Argentina, in Brazil, in China and in Spain, it is essential to know each other in order to do business together. These are high context societies. In these cultures, information is transmitted through the network.

Mexico
Interpersonal relations are very important in Mexico. The Mexicans tend to favour long-term relations based on mutual trust. One way to know a person is to know his family. Expertise is important but fitting into the group is probably equally important. The art of keeping up relations is therefore essential in Mexico.

Argentina
Maintaining good relations with your Argentinian interlocutor is a prerequisite for doing business. The new information technologies have an influence on the situation. Meetings always start and end with small conversations. It is therefore essential to plan this extra time in the agenda.

China
The Chinese are careful in business and like to establish relations before

concluding a deal. Several face-to-face appointments may be necessary before getting to the final stage of a negotiation. Here as well, establishing relations is a prerequisite for doing business.

Spain

In Spain, the network is very important. Indeed, in order to get a job, it is as important to be qualified as to have relations. Success in business much depends on personal contacts. For this reason, it is recommended to carefully choose your representatives.

Brazil

The Brazilians conduct business through personal connections. It is therefore relevant to hire the services of somebody who will make you meet the "right" people. It is not recommended to change your team in the course of a negotiation. This may ruin the whole process. The Brazilians tend to give more value to the person or the people with whom they do business than to the company they work for.

AU   US

In Australia and in the United States, it is not necessary to know each other on order to do business. These are low context societies. Information is segmented before being explicitly transmitted through "systematised" communication networks.

Conclusion

It may seem that getting ready for a negotiation is, all things considered, a rather universal endeavour. Nevertheless, the numerous examples provided in this chapter prove the opposite. There are many differences: the information sought is not always the same, neither are the sources...

In the field of intercultural negotiation, no strict method is effective. Only flexible modular approaches can work.

CHAPTER 5

HOW TO CONDUCT THE NEGOTIATION

"We must free ourselves of the hope that the sea will ever rest. We must learn to sail in high winds."
Aristotle Onassis

Subject: understanding the different aspects of an efficiently conducted negotiation.

There are many ways of conducting a negotiation and the best is always the most adapted to the context!

This chapter considers, in a logical way, the conduct of the negotiation in stages:

- How should you start the negotiation?
- How should you clarify the other party's real requests?
- How should you manage group dynamics?
- How should you make proposals?

First, the parties get to know each other. They set the framework, define it and make sure to build a common ground on which they will make their way. Then comes the differentiation stage, where the parties analyze their differences:

- How should you proceed with the negotiation?
- How should you respond to the other parties' proposals and reactions?

If you want to get results, you must join forces, which is exactly what happens during the integration stage. The parties come together and look for common solutions:

- How should you take a stand?

Starting the negotiation

It is said that the first ten minutes of a meeting are of crucial importance. The first impression is usually "lingering". For this reason, it is recommended to put all the winning cards on your side in order to start the negotiation in the best possible conditions (figure 5.1).

In some cultures (more generally in high context cultures such as in Egypt and Tunisia), meetings start with informal conversations. In other cultures (more generally in low context cultures), informal conversations are limited and don't have the same importance. It is for example the case in the United States, where negotiators tend to get more quickly to "the heart of the matter".

Establishing a common ground between the parties is of vital importance. In that respect, you shall focus on the other party's needs and determine the extent to which they coincide with your own needs. In this perspective, you shall avoid starting the negotiation with controversial issues. Once the common ground is established, you must keep developing and expanding it. It is usually the best way to find the most creative solutions suitable to all parties.

Do not forget to speak at a normal pace and, above all, to listen and observe.

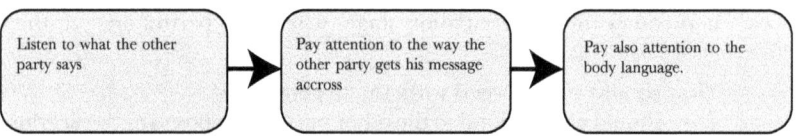

Figure 5.1 – Key elements at the start of a negotiation

Intercultural aspect of visual contacts

In some cultures (such as, amongst others, in the United States and in several Northern European countries), a frank and direct look is considered a sign of sincerity, as it generates trust. In contrast, in other cultures (such as in Japan), staring at somebody is considered rude or even aggressive and should therefore be avoided.

In some cultures and religious groups, a man and a woman staring at each other may be perceived as coming on to each other. Therefore, in these cultures, avoiding staring at people from the opposite sex is considered a sign of respect.

Cultures also differ in the amount of looks they consider as appropriate. Some experts make reference to this phenomenon by drawing a distinction between "high look" and "low look" cultures.

For example, the British culture is considered as "low look". Staring at people is perceived as invasive. In "high look" cultures, like for example in Italy, staring at others is perfectly acceptable and being seen is not a problem.

To sum up, in terms of visual contacts, it is essential to determine:
- the type of expected contacts and between which parties;
- the amount of looks accepted or expected.

Intercultural aspect of the notion of personal and public space

In some cultures, it is recommended to keep distance and to avoid most physical contacts. It is the case in many Asian countries, where you only touch close friends and relatives. For example, in Japan and in China, it is common for people to stand at more than one metre from one another. In contrast, in other cultures, interpersonal distance is much more limited and physical contacts are acceptable. It is the case in Argentina where interlocutors stand at a relatively close distance from one another. Stepping back can be considered insulting.

Case studies

Start of a negotiation between French and Japanese teams to discuss the manufacturing and marketing of a new series of toys for children

A Japanese and a French company meet to discuss the manufacturing and marketing of a new series of toys for children. Each delegation is made up of several members. The Japanese delegation is made up of members of different ages and backgrounds. The French delegation is also made up of people of different backgrounds. The senior member of the French team is called back for exceptional reasons. His colleagues take his place. It is obvious that the Japanese team reacts specifically to this relatively young team. France has a culture of debate in which everyone is invited to share their views. Things are different in Japan. The Japanese usually negotiate in teams made up of executives of different ages. Young executives often keep silent during negotiations. They nonetheless play an important part, particularly in terms of communication. Indeed, the Japanese like to transmit messages through young executives. For example: "My boss does not really like your offer". It is recommended to make sure there is at least one senior in your team and that this person is treated with respect.

First meeting between a German businessman and an Italian sales representative

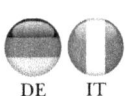

DE   IT

The meeting takes place in the foreign affairs department. The German businessman is considering setting up in Italy and wishes to better know the range of possibilities. After the greetings, the businessman starts the discussion in a precise and predefined order. His Italian counterpart looks rather disconcerted. The Italians like getting to know each other and discussing a while before talking business. They almost always prefer doing business with people they know, even if they only had a quick conversation with them.

It is often said that it takes less than 10 minutes for somebody to form an opinion but that it may take months to change it. So, it is better to start in the most appropriate way!

Presentation of a new product by a Belgian associate to a Chinese sister company

BE   CH

A Belgian engineer presents the features of a new product to be developed to the Chinese engineers who keep saying: "We have never done that before". The Belgian engineer lays emphasis on the innovative aspect of the idea and underlines that this product's development would mean a real competitive advantage. The Chinese engineers keep saying: "We have never done that before", which, to a Belgian engineer, is considered a clear refusal to go ahead.

The Chinese give great importance to the past. They consider seniority, tradition, age and other links to the past to be key values. Past experiences are often taken as example for present and future actions. Saying "We have never done that before" merely reflects this value.

The importance given to the past differs from one culture to the other. Westerners, such as the Americans, rather tend to favour the future and to seek innovation and novelty. Generally speaking, youth prevails over seniority, even more so at the professional level.

Thanks to the assistance of a Chinese colleague, the Belgian engineer better understands his Chinese counterparts and finally adapts his approach and arguments by making reference to the past and to existing models. Nevertheless, the strong value given to the past does not prevent the Chinese to be turned to the future!

Greetings in China

BE   CH

Interpersonal distance is interpreted differently from one culture to the other. In Belgium, kissing on the cheeks is merely a sign of friendship. In contrast, in China, kissing on the cheeks denotes love and is only tolerated in private.

In China, people only shake hands after being separated for a rather long time. Therefore, Chinese colleagues do not usually shake hands in the morning. In contrast, in Belgium, it is considered appropriate and polite to shake hands.

Starting a negotiation

IT

Meetings usually start with conversations. You do not get immediately to the heart of the matter. In Italy, being "technically" or "factually" prepared is not enough. You must also take the time to establish a relation of trust with your Italian counterparts, who like to make acquaintance and to discuss for a while before talking business. The Italians are hospitable. It may be sensible to hire a strong representative able to organise meetings and to introduce you to the right people.

TR

In Turkey, meetings start with long discussions and exchanges of information. You do not get immediately to the heart of the matter. The objective of these discussions is to get to know each other and to maintain good relations. It is necessary to establish good relations with your interlocutor before starting the negotiation and doing business. The majority of business is based upon interpersonal relations. Trust is seldom given to strangers and is rather reserved to family and close friends.

Importance of the greeting ritual in Indonesia

ID

More than anything else, greetings are very important and formal in Indonesia. Take your time. Hurrying things up would be considered as disrespectful and impolite.

Importance of the greeting ritual in Japan

JP

Bowing down is the traditional greeting in Japan. The depth of this movement reflects the type of relation you have. Keep the palms of your hands opened along your legs. Bowing as deep as your interlocutor is of crucial importance. The Japanese know the Western customs and will usually shake hands with you. This handshake is usually discreet (do not interpret it as a sign of your interlocutor's assertiveness) and longer than in European and North American countries. Titles are very important in Japan and must be respected.

Clarifying the real requests of the other party

You must quickly identify the other party's real requests. The usual reaction is to negotiate on the apparent requests. A much more efficient approach consists in understanding WHY the other party formulates such or such request. Or, in other terms, what interests is the other party trying to serve?

These interests correspond to the real request hidden behind the apparent one. The term "hidden" does not mean that the other party is trying to hide something from you. To him, the apparent request is merely the most appropriate to serve his own interests. The other party determines this request according to his knowledge of the situation, to his constraints, etc. If you have a better knowledge of his interests, it is possible to make him a more suitable offer which will also be in line with your own interests.

The notion of real request is of vital importance to avoid deadlock in a negotiation. Fisher and Ury[15] tell the story of two children negotiating the slicing of an orange. They each get half the fruit without realising that one of them only wanted the pulp while the other was only interested in the peel... It is therefore recommended not to focus on the apparent request but to try and determine what motivates it.

How can you determine the real request?

- Ask the question: The simplest solution is sometimes to ask directly the question. Keep your objectives in mind. The other parties must not have the feeling that you are asking them to justify themselves.
- Reformulate: in order to determine right from the start the other party's real request, you can try to give your initial request a broader perspective. In most cases, the other party starts the negotiation with an overvalued request. You should avoid focusing on a precise number or literally on the formulated demands. Otherwise, they might be considered as the starting point of the negotiation. You must broaden the debate.
- Put yourself in the other party's shoes: another approach consists in trying to put yourself in the other party's place. If you were him, what would be your constraints? What would you be trying to achieve or to avoid?
- Make reference to a third party: this method consists in asking explanations for the account of a third party, such as a superior authority.

After the analysis of real and apparent requests, you have to once again analyze the stakeholders' motivations. Motivations are what make the other parties act, independently from their objectives.

---

15 Fisher R., Ury W., *Getting to Yes. How to Negotiate Agreement without Giving In*, New York, Simon & Schuster, 1987.

Case studies

Clarifying the other party's requests

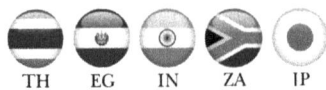
TH EG IN ZA IP

In Thailand, direct confrontation is always considered rude. Do not ask judgment questions such as: "According to you, which of these rival services is the best?" Be sharper and ask more indirect questions: "Which of these rival products do you use?" Avoid at all costs jumping to conclusions openly like, for example, by saying: "Does it mean you use this service because it is by far the best?" The answer may turn to be "yes" while it is not the case. People in Thailand would rather be evasive or find a credible excuse than openly answer "no". A flat refusal is seldom accepted and often considered rude. The same goes for Japan. In both countries, a smile may mean pleasure. It may also be a way of hiding anger, disapproval or embarrassment. Similar behaviours can be observed in Egypt, in India and in Saudi Arabia. If you want to determine the real request, you must go beyond appearances.

AT AU

In Austria, direct communication is appreciated. For example, in a conversation, the other party usually expects a strong and direct visual contact.

In the same fashion, the Australians appreciate and respect people having opinions and being able to express them. Do not hesitate to argue and stick to your line.

Managing group dynamics

A basic rule when dealing with a group is precisely not to consider it as a group but rather as a collection of individuals. It is in your interest to understand well what unites them but also what differentiate them from each other (figure 5.2).

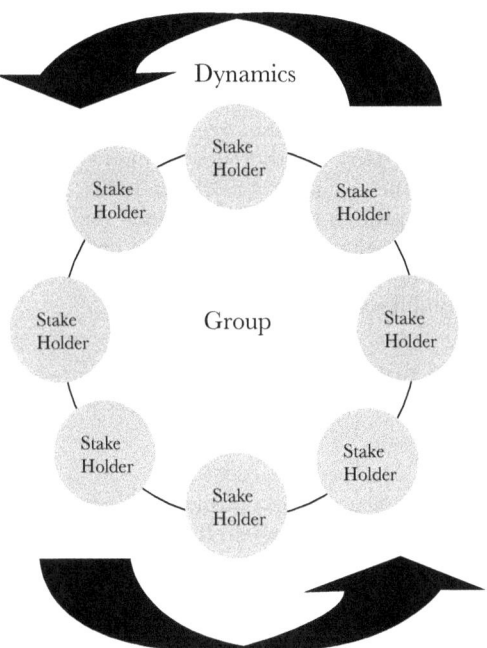

Figure 5.2 – Notion of group

It is recommended to identify a key stakeholder and, if possible, to make him an ally. Several factors will intervene in the choice of this special stakeholder:
- his influence over the negotiation team;
- your affinity with him;
- the balance between his objective and yours;
- etc.

Case studies

Discussion over a contract between a German aerospace company and its Belgian guidance system supplier

DE BE

The sales manager of an aerospace company meets his Belgian supplier of guidance system. Several major points were raised in previous meetings and the supplier would like to conclude the deal on this day. He looks rather annoyed with the "slowness" (so he perceives) of the process. In Germany, the decision making process is rather slow as many participants come into consideration. Once the decision is made, it is firm, even "irrevocable". The decision making process is very methodical. You should know that, in addition to the official command chain, German organisations usually have a parallel set of advisers and decision-makers. The approval of this "shadow cabinet" is often compulsory.

Congratulations in Indonesia

ID

In Indonesia, individuals are seldom pushed to the front in public, whether for being congratulated or reprimanded. If you have to reprimand somebody, always do it quietly and in private. It is of vital importance in terms of group dynamics.

Presentation of a project in China

CH

China is a country where the hierarchical distance is rather important but where each group or subgroup is relevant. Therefore, when starting projects, be prepared to make presentations to several groups of interlocutors.

Group dynamics in India

IN

Although there are many religions in India, the country does not have an official one. Religion plays a major part in everyday life. A majority of Indians are Hindus. Hinduism is polytheistic. The belief in Karma and in reincarnation is of fundamental importance. In order to escape the reincarnation's cycles and to reach nirvana, you must apply the principle of non intervention to humanity and stop interfering with your actions. The caste system in India is supported by the majority of variants of Hinduism. The origin of this system is obscure. It has been existing for thousands of years in India. Although the government declared caste discrimination illegal, castes still play a significant part in politics and business in the country. There are traditionally four castes, but these are subdivided in thousands of sub-castes. These elements influence group dynamics in many ways.

Making proposals

In negotiation, it is necessary to identify which proposal you are going to put forward, as well as how and when you are going to do it. You also have to decide who is going to make the first proposal (table 5.1).

Table 5.1 – Things to do and to be avoided when making proposals

At this stage, it is recommended to…	At this stage, it is recommended to avoid…
Carefully listen to the other party. His position may be unexpectedly similar to yours.	Making too many concessions at the start of the negotiation.
Write down all proposals word for word.	Making inflexible offers. It would then prove more difficult to backtrack without losing face.
Keep room for manoeuvre (the first proposal is usually considered by the parties as a basic offer open to improvement. This first offer must enable you to see how the land lies).	Using radical words such as "never", "impossible"…

At this stage, it is recommended to...	At this stage, it is recommended to avoid...
Set the conditions of your offer ("if... then...").	Answering questions merely by "yes" or "no"
Keep the opportunity to refuse an offer if necessary.	Talking if you do not have anything relevant to say.
Ask the other party's **opinion**.	
Stand ready to switch strategy if reaching an agreement at the beginning of the negotiation is possible	

The way you present a proposal is important, as it is a culturally responsive point. For example, timidity may be considered an asset in Sweden, while in Russia, on the other hand, being assertive and direct is recommended. It is nonetheless advised to adopt in all cases an open and firm physical posture and to put forward your arguments with confidence.

Examples

In Germany, business proposals are preferably presented in a rational and structured manner, going by concrete facts and, in some cases, statistics.

In Brazil, facts also matter, but communication modes are somehow different. The information is preferably transmitted orally, going by visual elements.

Case studies

Making trade proposals

AR AU

In Argentina, tolerance to uncertainty is considered to be relatively low, which translates into a certain aversion to risk. The Argentinians have the reputation of being tough negotiators. Aversion to risk leads undoubtedly to stillness. It is important to bear this fact in mind when drawing up and putting forward proposals. Present your arguments with confidence and cast-iron evidence.

In contrast, in Australia, tolerance to risk is rather high, which translates, amongst others, into the quick adoption of new technologies and methods. Science, external structures, the nuclear family, etc. are sources of stability. If there is anxiety, it is rather developed at the personal level and connected to the ability to fulfill some obligations and to achieve certain results. Once again, taking into account the participants' relation to risk enables you to better organise and communicate your proposals. You should adopt an innovative approach.

Impact of orientation (to dialogue or to data) on the communication of proposals

RU UK CA

Russia is dialogue-oriented. Specific importance is given to communication between people. In this type of environment, establishing and maintaining relations is of crucial importance. It is necessary to go beyond the factual stage, which is only of relative importance. Therefore, when putting forward proposals and arguments, your relations must be as strong as possible.

In contrast, in data-oriented cultures, like in the United Kingdom and in Canada, the emphasis is laid on the accuracy and relevance of the provided information. Expectations stand at a rather factual level. Therefore, when putting forward proposals and arguments, the content must be accurate and relevant.

This point must be taken into account in order to make proposals at the right time and in the right way.

Making progress in the negotiation

You have to identify the levers which will enable you to get things moving and to achieve the expected results:
- should you go through bureaucratic channels or should you go for innovation?
- should you make reference to change or should you encourage stability?
- etc.

Identifying these levers enables you to determine the rules of the game in order to, in fine, make the most of them.

How to make progress in the negotiation according to the type of company you are in

Quinn[16] determines four types of organisational cultures through the juxtaposition of these two dimensions:
- 1st dimension: stability versus change:
- 2nd dimension: internal orientation versus external orientation.

Quinn's model is based on the postulate that organisations can be characterised according to features or dimensions which are common to all human organisations ("universal cultural features"). This model focuses more specifically on tensions and conflicts inherent to organisations (figure 5.3).

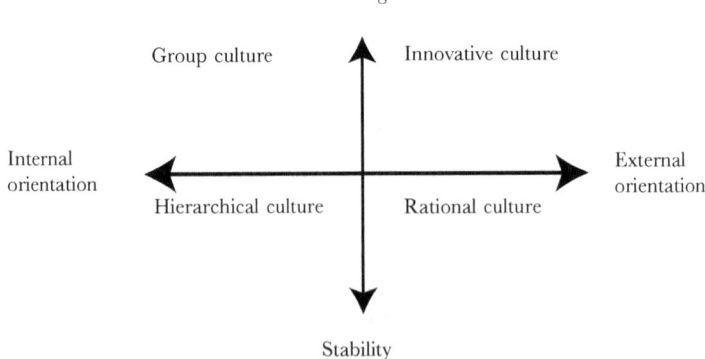

Figure 5.3 – Quinn's organisational analysis model

---

16 Cameron K.S., Quinn R.E., *Diagnosing and Changing Organizational Culture: Based on the Competing Values Framework*, Prentice Hall, 1999.

These four types of organisational cultures are "ideal types". It is rather unlikely for an organisation to only feature one of these types. Organisations are made of combinations. The coexistence of prevailing conflicting values may trigger internal tensions.

Example of a source of progress in negotiation according to the types of organisational culture

Let us take the example of a project manager working for a German public corporation. Had this corporation to be classified, it may be said it has a both rational and hierarchical culture. In order to bring a project to a satisfactory conclusion in such an environment, you must use statistics (it would be pointless to put forward a project based on impressions) and respect the hierarchy. In this system, you must go by the existing rules.

Let us take the example of another project manager working for a French new media company. In that case, you are halfway between group culture and innovative culture. New media companies are, by nature, more innovation-oriented. As we already found out, the notion of network is essential in France. In order to bring a project to a satisfactory conclusion in such an environment, you have to be innovative in the presentation of projects but also to present them to the right people and activate the network. A person with good connections talks to another, who may in turn talk to a third one... This is how many projects see the light of day, while others are discarded.

Table 5.2. Description of the organisations identified by Quinn

	Group culture	Innovative culture	Hierarchical culture	Rational culture
Strategic view	Orientation to human resources development.	Orientation to innovation, growth and resources acquisition.	Stability-orientation, continuity, enforcement of rules and procedures	Orientation to competitive advantage and superiority on the market
Basic values	Participation, trust and feeling of belonging to a family.	Dynamism, adaptability, creativity and entrepreneurship.	Order, rules, uniformity, internal efficiency and assessment.	Competitiveness, objectives achievement and productivity.
Main factors of motivation	Social cohesion, ethics and tradition.	Growth, risk, creativity, reaction and action.	Stability, security, permanence and procedures.	Achievement of measurable objectives and competition.
Leadership style	Participative leadership favouring interactions through team work.	The leader is an entrepreneur inclined to take risks.	The leader is a manager, an organiser and an administrator.	Authoritarian leadership; the leader is an expert; he determines productivity and the objectives to achieve.
Efficiency criteria	Development of human potential and fairness towards members.	Growth, development of new markets and resources acquisition.	Control, stability and efficiency.	Planning, productivity and efficiency.
Source of progress in the negotiation	Using the network	Using Innovative spirit.	Going through hierarchical channels	Using statistics

Case studies

Progress assessment of a project

FR   CH

A product is being developed. For the French, the process is running smooth: choice of technical platform, marketing specifications, technical feasibility analysis, development, integration, tests and marketing. It was decided that the development would take place in China. During a meeting, the French mention a risk linked to the components cost which should be watched closely. Failing to do so may call into question the product profitability. The Chinese management asks immediately for an analysis in order to choose a cheaper platform. For the French, given that the choice of platform is an upstream process, it was unthinkable to go back to this step at such an advanced stage of the project. This would have meant stopping the project and starting a new one. There was much emotion on the French side and the Chinese team continued with the project while at the same time assessing the possibility of using a new platform. Finally, the initial platform was chosen.

Individuals do not use their time in the same way. While monochronic people would rather deal with one activity at a time, polychronic people prefer managing several activities at the same time. Monochronic and polychronic times have a bearing on the way people organise themselves. For example, in monochronic cultures, once a project is approved, it is conducted in accordance with the established modalities and planning. Any event may call into question the expected development of the project.

The time factor must be taken into consideration in the assessment of a negotiation progress.

Choosing between oral and written communication: use of memos and specification documents

BE   CH   FR

A Belgian employee in mission to China writes down, during her whole stay, all the facts and decisions taken. She writes several memos and specification documents which she shares with the participants to the project. At the end of her stay, she compiles for the project manager a summary detailing all points addressed and decisions taken. During her second stay in China, the manager of the "professional products" department asks her to validate one by one all the components which must be integrated to the product. This list appears in one of the specification documents handed out during the last stay, which was also updated and sent by email. Chemical engineers join the discussion. They also ask questions which were already answered in the previously sent documents. When the Belgian employee points that out, she realises they never heard of these documents.

The transmission of written information is clearly less developed in China that in Belgium. Projects can be developed because people talk to each other, not because they write to each other.

While observing her Chinese colleagues during the meetings, the Belgian employee realises that they often show up without bringing any paper, which would be inconceivable in Belgium or in France. Somebody showing up to a meeting without paper, bringing along a mere pen, would be at best considered a tourist.

The fact that the Chinese writing is less efficient than our alphabet and was in the past only accessible to a limited number of people partially explains why oral communication is privileged.

It is important to choose appropriate tools in order to get a negotiation further.

Choosing between oral and written communication: work on site versus remote work

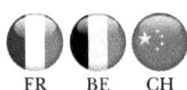

A Franco-Belgian cosmetics company decides to launch a new series of products with the support of its Chinese subsidiary. During the project, the Chinese team complains several times because it does not get from France the necessary resources and support for the good development of the project. They are asking for the physical presence of all the parties. The Franco-Belgian answer stays the same: "You can work at a distance; you have all the means available to exchange information." For the Chinese, the problem remains the same and they keep asking for the presence of their French colleagues. From the Chinese point of view, the success of a project depends on the quality of communication between the team members, which should mainly be oral. In practice, only a limited number of team members, those working regularly with the Franco-Belgian office, communicate in writing.

Choosing between oral and written communication: the purchasing function

FR   CH

French buyers are used to consult several providers on the basis of written specifications. Once the answers have been received, they choose the most relevant and start negotiating. After several weeks, again on the basis of written and negotiated offers, they announce the final choice to the project manager who will then set the required technical options. The notion of purchasing is very different in China. Chinese engineers needing a component for a project call directly the providers on the phone and see them shortly after – between a few hours and two days – and start negotiating technical features and prices orally. They choose the component and send its reference along with the provider's name to the supplies department who will further negotiate.

Confronted with the Chinese methods which partially deprive them from their negotiating power, some French buyers call it a scandal. They consider it a lack of maturity in the way they manage providers which is confirmed, according to them, by the higher prices their Chinese colleagues get. Confronted with the slowness of the French purchasing procedures, the Chinese engineers also call it a scandal, as it creates delays of several weeks. This translates into a waste of production time and, therefore, into a loss of profitability.

The economic loss induced by both methods is not easily perceptible, and each method has pros and cons. Trying to determine who is wrong or right would be tricky and rather untimely.

Responding to the other party's proposals and reactions

When answering a proposal, it is recommended to observe some basic rules:

- *avoiding responding too quickly* to a proposal! This might weaken your position;
- *rephrasing* the other party's proposal in order to make sure that everybody has the same understanding of it. To this end, use sentences such as: "If I got it right…" "Can you guarantee us that…?";

- *showing* the other party *your willingness to reach a compromise*. This point is of crucial importance. That being said, do not make "free" or "anonymous" concessions.
- *allowing yourself some time to think* after each important proposal;
- laying emphasis on the *similarities* between your proposal and the other party's;
- suggesting, if necessary, *alternatives* in line with the other party's needs and priorities;
- *listening to the other party*. In a majority of cases, it is recommended not to interrupt the other party and to let him put forward his arguments, proposals or comments, even though this point is culturally responsive. For example, in so-called polychronic cultures like Brazil, conversations are not linear and interruptions are much more frequent. On the other hand, in monochronic cultures, interruptions are rather unwelcome.

Some tactics to save time

There is a vast number of tactics to save time. Some have negative impacts on the other party, some others don't. Here are some examples of tactics from the second category:

- asking the other party to provide details on a specific subject or asking questions in the aim of focusing the debate on a specific point;
- broadening the negotiation scope by asking additional questions;
- asking to interrupt the meeting in order to ask the opinion and/or assistance of a third party or colleague, or even to report to an external authority.

Responding to the other party's reactions

In some cases, the other party may use "stratagems" to influence you. The term stratagem implies the notion of "manipulation". You must be able to identify these stratagems and to deal with them in a controlled manner. The main purposes of these manipulations are:

- to divide the attention of your group members in order to better control the debate;
- to take your attention as far away from the negotiation main subject as possible in order to more easily rephrase the terms of the agreement:
- to manipulate your team in order to conclude the negotiation before it is completely satisfied.

Table 5.3 – Examples of stratagems commonly used in negotiation and examples of reactions to these tactics

	Manipulation	Examples of reactions
Threat	Presenting an array of negative consequences in case the terms of the proposal would not be accepted. Laying emphasis on the potential risks of loss.	Making it clear to the other party that you do not negotiate under pressure. Assessing other possibilities.
Offend	Calling into question the performance of the group members. Criticising products, services, people…	Keeping calm and not being emotional. Reaffirming your position and letting the other party know that the negotiation will be over if he/she does not adopt a more constructive attitude.
Bluff	Threatening of vague retaliation. Making unfounded assertions (for example the competition is willing to pay more for the product on sale).	Cleverly denouncing the bluff, directly or indirectly. Refuting the other party's assertions and wait for his reaction. Asking details on, and/or proofs of the points on which you have doubts.
Intimidation	Making people wait. Seating on a more comfortable chair than the other party.	Deactivating the other party's stratagems aiming solely at destabilising trust. Never giving anything without compensation. Letting no one force you to accept an unsuitable agreement.
"Divide and rule"	Exploiting disagreements in the other group by regularly calling upon the member who favours you the most.	Contemplating this situation with the group beforehand and defining the attitudes to adopt in such circumstances. Asking the adjournment of the negotiation if the disagreement is too deep.

	Manipulation	Examples of reactions
Treacherous questions	Asking lots of question in order to lay emphasis on the other party's weaknesses and to force him to make concessions.	Avoiding answering these questions when the intentions are clear. Do not hesitate to mention if it is out of the subject. Checking every request of the other party. Setting conditions to the proposals you make.
Arousing emotions	Insinuating that people are not being honest. Insisting on all concessions and sacrifices made. Saying that you are offended by the lack of trust.	Asserting your willingness to reach a win-win agreement. Asking questions to check the validity of the requests. Concentrating on the subjects which have to be negotiated.
Limits test	Getting additional concessions through minor changes in the contract terms in order to get longer-term benefits.	After each agreement, write down clearly: – the approved elements. – the commitment on both sides.

If you realise you were caught out in one of the other party's stratagems, you should take the time to think before giving an answer.

Avoiding emotional reactions

Following an a participant's emotional reaction, the negotiation may develop very quickly. These emotional reactions have different origins:
- they may be the result of unstable, confuse or aggressive feelings or of a lack of self-control;
- they may also be part of a conscious stratagem (it is important to learn to detect this kind of methods in order to discourage the other party to use this strategy again in the future).

Table 5.4 – Examples of cases where the debate needs to be refocused

Problem	Possible reactions
Confused negotiator	Clarifying critical points, which are source of confusion. Writing down complex proposals (short and straight to the point). Sticking to the agenda to a certain extent in order to avoid additional confusions in the future. Being ready to involve a third party to review the points discussed from a new angle.
Change of negotiator	Progressing calmly and systematically. Not hesitating to go through points already addressed if necessary. Promising to sum up the points already addressed at a predefined time. Postponing the session so that the new negotiator can find out his team's opinion. Trying to present points already addressed in a different way.
Emotional negotiator	Avoiding calling into question systematically the negotiator's intentions or integrity. Not interrupting the negotiator and waiting for him to finish before answering. Asking a rational question for each emotional reaction. Adjourning the session in order to give the negotiator time to calm down.
Aggressive negotiator	Repeating calmly the points mentioned and avoiding showing your emotions. Keeping clear from angry words and staying calm. Pointing out firmly that you do not accept intimidation attempts, acts of violence or threats. Suggesting an adjournment in order for everybody to calm down.

In some cases, adjourning the session may be beneficial: to get over very strong emotional reactions, to save time, when brand new elements are introduced in the debate... However, note that an adjournment delays the conclusion of a negotiation. This technique must therefore be used sparingly. If however you have to ask for an adjournment, make sure to note down exactly where the negotiation was interrupted.

Case studies

Notion of compromise

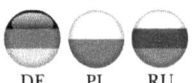
DE   PL   RU

German negotiators can be very assertive. Being forced to make a compromise may be considered a personal failure. The same goes for Poland and Russia, where being tough is a source of pride.

In some countries, people tend to answer "yes" to any question. It is the opposite in the case of Russia, even though things are changing with the coming of the new generation. Why did Russian executives tend to refuse many business proposals? First, innovation was by and large discouraged. Then, people were afraid of being held responsible in case of failure. Finally, it was often the sole power of bureaucrats. Indeed, while it is very difficult to find an individual having the power to support a whole project by his own, it is common to find individuals able to block everything on their own.

Even more here than in other cultures, it is important not to make free compromise and, above all, to get better in this area.

Establishment of a joint venture between two aeronautical companies to develop a "green" plane prototype

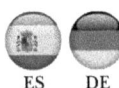
ES   DE

The two managers of a Spanish and a German company meet to discuss a potential partnership on an aeronautical project to develop a "green" plane prototype. This costly development needs multiple financial and technical contributions. The negotiation is in progress. The Spanish representative goes back over a point previously addressed. The German representative points out that this point was already discussed and that it would be untimely to go back over it. The Spanish culture is polychronic, not linear. It is perfectly acceptable to go back over a point already addressed while you are still in the cycle. It is much less the case in the rather monochronic German culture, in which time is considered to be rather linear. The time factor must be taken into consideration in order to react in the most appropriate way.

Taking a stand

At this stage, you regularly sum up and reaffirm your position. This must be done calmly and without being aggressive. Laying emphasis on the positive elements enables you to reduce the impact of negative elements on the negotiation. If you make a mistake, it is sometimes more effective to immediately admit to it, directly or indirectly, than waiting. However that may be, it must never lead you to lose face. Finally, always bear in mind your initial objectives.

It is recommended to regularly put the relevance of the other party's argument to the test: interpretation of figures, presentation of facts... Whatever the situation, personal attacks are always counter-productive and shall be avoided.

At this stage, the other party may have the temptation to try and weaken your position in order to influence the balance of powers. It is important to be able to identify this type of tactics, which can be financial, legal, social or even based on emotions (table 5.5).

Table 5.5 – Additional examples of tactics to influence the balance of power

Financial	Consists in imposing expenses to the other party in case no agreement is reached.
Legal	Consists in establishing a legal framework discouraging the other party to consider certain cases which would be detrimental to you.
Social	Consists in imposing restrictions based on ethical grounds.
Based on emotions	Consists in holding the other party responsible for the situation and, generally speaking, in playing on people's emotions.

Case studies

Taking a stand in China

CH   ID

In this area, it is essential to understand what lies behind an apparent approval or disapproval.

China and Indonesia have rather collectivist cultures. It means that members of a same culture are likely to support each other, which is often the case even if a proposal or argument is far from being perfect. There is a certain notion of solidarity. This element must be taken into account when analysing the other party's reactions. The opinions may not be all that different. Understanding this point and using this knowledge will enable you to make progress in the negotiation.

Conclusion

One of the main mistakes in negotiation is to elude the differentiation and integration stages and to hastily jump on solutions, without exactly getting the scope of the situation. It is even more the case in intercultural negotiation, where things are not always what they seem.

The many examples given in this chapter remind us that for a negotiation to be successful, it is necessary to work on the content but as well (at least as important) on the container (or process), i.e. taking habits and customs into account, talking to the right people, etc. This point could not be stressed enough!

CHAPTER 6

HOW TO CLOSE THE NEGOTIATION PLAN FOR THE FUTURE

"Capital isn't scarce; vision is."
Sam Walton

Subject: understanding how to pass from the "in progress" stage to the final stage.

Closing the negotiation is a key step. It is the compromise stage. You must choose carefully the time and the way to close a negotiation. An inappropriate choice may prove extremely damaging. This stage is full of emotions. The end of the negotiation is close. In one way or another, the parties will have to close the debates and agree on a final outcome. At this stage, it is important to consider the means of implementing the agreement and to make sure the latter will be respected.

In this chapter, two cases are considered: concluding the negotiation by yourself and concluding the negotiation in association with one or several third parties.

This chapter considers the closing of the negotiation as follows:
- How should you make sure major problems are resolved?
- How should you start the conclusion?
- How should you make a last offer and go beyond the potential reluctance of the other parties?
- How should you implement the decisions taken?
- How should you consider future prospects?

Concluding the negotiation by yourself

Make sure major problems are resolved

You must make sure all main problems are resolved. Leaving some problems till the end (to save time or for any other reason) would be a major strategic mistake. Make sure as well that all the parties understand the points of view. To this end, it is better to use a common language. If necessary, do not hesitate to suggest that the main terms of the agreement be precisely defined, which will enable you to avoid bad surprises and potential misunderstandings.

Case studies

Development and marketing of a new Sino-French product

FR   CH

Let us take the example of the development and marketing of a new Sino-French product. The French team spends several weeks defining the market targets, the consumers' profile, the product features, etc. A this stage, the Chinese company don't even have the necessary teams to perform this work. There are only the project teams, which will develop the product. During this time of investigation, the Chinese team is much impatient to start manufacturing the product. To the question: "On which day will you be able to give us the first model of the product?", the answer "We first have to precisely determine our consumer targets before finalising a product" leaves the Chinese speechless. Theirs remarks on the time to market which is not respected wax eloquent on the way they perceive the French rhythm.

The project approach is much different in China than in France. The French first imagine a theory, plan things carefully and then start the development stage by following their theory as much as possible. The Chinese will get directly to the heart of the matter and do the best they can with the available means. They do not spend much time on the theoretical aspects before getting to the practical ones. As the project proceeds, their choices will have to be optimised according to the environment.

In the French approach, how is it possible to make sure that major problems are resolved? In China, "major problems" are resolved throughout the process and, therefore, are less considered as "major". It is therefore necessary to first "forget" this approach. It is recommended to have a kind of scoreboard and to permanently follow-up current activities and their progress.

Starting the conclusion

The list in table 6.1 (overleaf) is not exhaustive and may be considered as a compilation of suggestions to close a negotiation.

As soon as the best way of concluding a negotiation is identified, you must choose the most appropriate time to make your final proposal. Choose preferably an optimistic time of the negotiation.

Table 6.1 – Methods to conclude a negotiation

Group culture	Elements to be considered
Putting forward concessions suitable to all	This method may help you to get out of a predicament or "dead-end". It can also lead the other party to make more concessions than he/she would under other circumstances. You should nonetheless bear in mind that making concessions at the end of a process can, in some cases, have a negative impact on your credibility.
Meeting halfway	Note that in some cases, it may be difficult to strike the right balance in terms of advantages and disadvantages between the parties. This method implies that you are ready to make concessions. This method favours win-win situations.
Giving one of the parties the possibility to choose between two reasonable solutions	Using this method needs creativity. Finding two reasonable and attractive solutions is indeed not always easy. This method has a major disadvantage: It leads you to reveal your "game". Nevertheless, it has a major advantage: it enables you (by reducing the number of options) to strongly influence the orientation of the negotiation.

6. How to close the negotiation and plan for the future

Table 6.1 (contd) – Methods to conclude a negotiation

Group culture	Elements to be considered
Putting forward a new system of rewards or, alternatively, of penalties. Changing the stakes and putting some "pressure" on the other party by introducing new rewards or penalties.	You should know that the threat of being penalised may be considered as a sign of hostility by the other party. It is recommended to underline the fact that new advantages may have favourable impacts on the other party's situation and influence the balance of powers. Advantage of this method: in some cases, it gives momentum to the other party and enables you to reach an agreement more quickly.
Introducing new facts and elements at a late stage of the process. Introducing new facts and elements may, in some cases, encourage discussions and lead to an agreement.	This method may enable the other party to widen the scope of the negotiations and consider new possibilities. Nevertheless, using this method may have a negative impact on your credibility. The other party may consider that these elements could have been communicated earlier. Using this method can also have a negative impact on the basis of the negotiation. This would take the parties back to square one or, at least, back to an earlier stage of the negotiation process.
Suggesting an adjournment if you reach a so-called "dead-end" situation. An adjournment can be, for all the parties, a good opportunity to consider the consequences in case no agreement would be reached.	This method enables all the parties to ask the opinion of one or several people not participating to the debate. Before using this method, bear in mind that some circumstances may, in the meantime, change the state of affairs and lead the parties to reconsider their positions. It is therefore, in some respects, "a double-edged sword". Note a practical point: it may prove difficult to find a new date for the next meeting. It is even more the case if there are many participants.

Case studies

Tactics to start a conclusion

TR

In Turkey, the level of tolerance to uncertainty is rather low. Laws and rules structure the vision of the world. Tactics aiming at reducing uncertainty may prove efficient. In this area, giving one of the parties the opportunity to choose between two reasonable solutions or putting forward a system of penalties are common practices. Trying to reduce uncertainty is both a good lever and a most convincing argument. Say for example: "The proposal put forward is sound and safe. Other solutions could be imagined, but would these be as reliable on the long-term?"

Making your final offer and overcoming the possible reluctance of the other parties

Making your final offer

It is essential to choose the most appropriate time to make your last offer: a good proposal coming at the wrong time may be refused. Create a favourable atmosphere and make your final offer at a time the other party is most receptive.

> <u>Ways to create a positive atmosphere:</u>
> - Pushing the other party forward: "Very good arguments. I can therefore offer you…"
> - Laying emphasis on the work done together: "Today, we have done a remarkable work, and I offer you…"

It is also essential to choose the most appropriate way to make your last offer: during the negotiation, an offer may have been presented several times as a "last offer". It is a commonly used tactic. However, unless you are sure this offer is final, use other tactics as well. Using this tactic unwisely creates an unreliable climate. Should this happen, you can say that you would rather not conclude an agreement than make more compromises.

Formulating your last offer: you must make your offer calmly and firmly, while clearly indicating it is the final one. Here are some examples of sentences you can use to this end:
- "The management won't let me make another proposal";
- "This is my last offer, and I can't go further…";
- "I already offered more than I had planned".

Encouraging the other party to close the negotiation

In the event the other party would not accept your proposal, try to understand why. You can also invite the other party to make a proposal he considers suitable.

Table 6.2 – Methods to encourage the other party to reach a conclusion

Method		Consequences of using this method
Laying emphasis on the advantages	According to the circumstances, present all the advantages of the other party's proposal. However, avoid making reference to the advantages for you.	This method enables the other party to consider his offer from a new angle and creates win-win situations.
Encouraging the other party	Encourage the other party for each constructive proposal, even if that comes late… If the proposal does not suit you, it will always be possible to turn it down later in the negotiation process.	This method creates a positive atmosphere between the parties. It enables you to avoid criticisms linked to your own proposals anad to avoid creating a conflict over a critical point of the debate.

Method		Consequences of using this method
Avoiding win-lose situations	Insist on the fact that you want to reach a fair agreement. Do not force the other party to accept an agreement which he/she might consider as being imposed on him.	This method enables you to avoid confrontations which might create hostility and bring the negotiation to a halt. It allows maintaining an atmosphere favourable to constructive discussions and, therefore, to make counter-proposals more easily.
Helping the other party to save face	Come up with excuses that the other party can use to save face. Use for example hypothetical questions or proposals: "What would you think if...", What would you say if..."	This method tends to make the other party more accommodating. In that way, your proposals are more likely to be accepted. It reduces pressure on the other party, who accepts or refuses the proposal. Decisions can therefore be taken more quickly.

The closer you get to the final decision, the more people around the negotiation table become nervous. You must find a way to go beyond the other party's last hesitation. The time between the verbal agreement and the signature of the contract is particularly delicate. Under pressure, some negotiators tend to change their minds. If you feel that the other party hasn't made up his mind yet, it may be useful to remind him/her that this deal is going to lead to major changes for you to. If the other party is still hesitating, and that you are in a position of strength, you can always impose the agreement. Nevertheless, this method is not recommended. It may, amongst other things, have negative impacts in the future if you come to negotiate with the same people or with other parties connected to them.

At this stage more than ever, you must work in a "spirit of compromise". It does not necessarily mean you should accept too quickly the other party's proposals. If the session has to be adjourned, make sure to set a new date as soon as possible to go through the several options considered to break the deadlock.

Case studies

How should you make your last offer

RU

In Russia, being assertive is essential. It is a mark of quality and a proof of strength. Take this element into account when presenting your offers and even more when comes the time to make your last one. Be resolute.

US

The United States are data-oriented. If you want to get things to progress, it is recommended to use concrete and short-term oriented data.

Choosing the appropriate time to make your last offer

CH   ID

The case below indicates the most appropriate time to make your last offer. In China or in Indonesia, people strongly believe in luck and in the influence of external forces on their lives. Some Chinese and Indonesians will refuse to take important decisions if the day is not considered favourable.

Concluding the negotiation with the support of one or more third parties

Negotiations may be interrupted for several reasons (for example if somebody leaves the table). In that case, you will have to act quickly to prevent the situation to get worse. The more you wait, the more the parties may be filled with bitterness.

Major advice at this stage:
- limit the damage by restoring a positive communication as quickly as possible: it is better to act during the meeting. However, if the bitterness is too strong, it is better to start reconciliation at a later time;

- resolve major disagreements: if an individual decides to leave the meeting alone, persuade his colleagues to convince him to come back. If the whole team leaves the table, you can ask the member of your team having the best relation with the other parties to try and bring them back to the negotiation table. You may also call upon a third party.

Calling upon a third party

In some cases, it is recommended to call upon a third party to conclude a negotiation. There are two main options:
- calling upon a mediator if the parties are willing to continue discussions;
- going to arbitration if the negotiations are completely broken off.

▶ Mediation

It is recommended to call upon a mediator when the parties to the negotiation have the feeling of having gone through all possibilities without reaching a suitable solution. The parties must show their willingness to get the negotiations back on course by accepting the mediator. Note that calling upon a mediator is a costly solution which should therefore be avoided if possible.

Mediation is a principle according to which a neutral individual is called upon in order to get things moving again between several parties. This neutral individual is in charge of identifying possible solutions so that the parties can reach a common agreement.

Mediator's role:
- being impartial;
- considering the situation from different angles;
- helping the parties to understand each other;
- explaining major problems and critical points to all the parties;
- suggesting new possible solutions;
- helping the parties to find a solution recognised by all.

Selection criteria:
- the mediator must be recognised by all the parties;
- it would be tempting to choose an expert in the area, somebody who would have much influence given his status. Bear in mind that the mediator's role is to put forward solutions. In that sense, it may be more

appropriate to choose somebody less reputable, and who would not have pre-formed opinions on the matters at hand. Indeed, the mediator must be able to make varied suggestions in order to break the deadlock.

▸ Arbitration

In the case of negotiations breaking off, arbitration is also a possibility. It implies involving a third party. This person will determine the solution to be adopted by all he parties in order to break the deadlock.

The arbitrator's role:
- being a reliable source of information;
- remaining impartial through the whole negotiation process;
- helping the parties to find a solution acceptable to all;
- taking into account every aspect of the problem which lead to the deadlock;
- if necessary, taking decisions authenticated through legal procedures.

The arbitrator has a major advantage over the mediator: he has the authority to force the parties to remain on the negotiation table until they reach an agreement.

Implementing decisions

Once an agreement is concluded, the decisions will have to be implemented. To this end, it is recommended to set up an implementation plan and to entrust it to selected people:
- the implementation plan must be validated by all the parties;
- it is essential to officially appoint one or several people in charge of the good development of the implementation plan;
- the implementation tasks should ideally be entrusted to people according to their experience and aptitudes;
- define right from the start the means of implementation in case of delay or any other problem.

Note that, in terms of implementation, the trend is different from one culture to the other. In cultures where the prevailing managerial logic is the logic of contract (it is the case of Germany), the trend is to implement the agreement according to the contract terms. In cultures where the prevailing managerial logic is the logic of honour, the contract terms will also be respected, but keeping your word will be considered at least as important.

Case studies

Comparing the meaning of agreements in France, in China, in Germany, in Sweden and in the United States

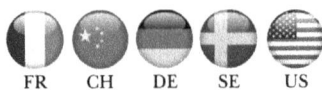

FR   CH   DE   SE   US

In order to implement an agreement, it is necessary to define its scope. Are the terms of this agreement strict or flexible? For example, the way time is perceived and used has an impact on the way an agreement is implemented. The Germans, the Swedish and the Americans have a much more linear perception of time than the French, and even more than the Chinese who have a cyclical perception of time.

Once the specifications are determined and accepted, or once the contract is signed, the Americans, the Germans and the Swedish attach great importance to developing what was concluded according to the chosen methods. Things happen in a linear way, with a past, a present and a future. It is already less the case for the French. Modifications and other revisions of the project are acceptable. For the German, that would mean re-examining the contract and its means of implementation. In some respect, the French are also polychronic, particularly when it comes to their flexibility in terms of schedules, planning and delivery dates.

Meaning of contracts

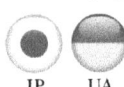

IP   UA

In Japan, a contract is not considered the end of the agreement. The parties still have the possibility to negotiate after its signature. In contrast, in Ukraine, a deal is only sealed when a contract is signed. Once the agreement is sealed, do not expect to further negotiate.

Implementation of the agreement

UK

In the United Kingdom, the prevailing managerial logic is the logic of contract. A certain amount of time is dedicated to the drafting of the contract terms which will be implemented (or at least be applicable) point by point.

Relation to uncertainty and implementation of the agreement

DE

In Germany, once an agreement is made, project teams take over. The agreement is implemented in accordance with its terms. Any change is usually considered a modification of the initial agreement or even a new agreement.

Some examples of decision making

AR BR TH DE UK JP SE ID

- *In Argentina, in Brazil and in Thailand, decisions are taken by one individual in the interest of the whole group.*

    In Argentina, decisions are usually taken by a high-ranking individual, in the interest of the community. Friendships and relations play a significant part in decision making. You should know that until the contract signature, any element is likely to be renegotiated.

    In Brazil, relations and personal feelings are, together with facts and ideologies, part of the decision making. Individuals are responsible for their actions but it should be underlined that loyalty to family is one of the most important duties. Family is by far the most important institution in Brazil.

    In Thailand, decisions are taken centrally. The typical decision maker is authoritarian, benevolent and takes his decisions in an autonomous way. The typical subordinate is respectful and obedient. Most people in Thailand are non-assertive and aware of both other's feelings and their position in society.

- *In Germany and in the United Kingdom, decisions are taken by an individual in accordance with rules and in respect of the group.*

    The English and the Germans are rather individualistic. Decisions are taken by individuals but always within the scope of the family, the group, the organisation. Individual initiatives and achievements are pushed forward, leading to significant personal leadership.

- *In Japan, in Sweden and in Indonesia, decisions are rather taken by consensus.*

    In Japan, the search for consensus is essential in the decision making process. Therefore, individuals sometimes have to reconsider their positions. The Japanese are moderately collective. In Sweden, most people prefer to make decisions by consensus. This process may nonetheless be very subtle, as participants express their opinions and feelings through signs, for example by looking or nodding at each other.

In Indonesia, decisions are traditionally taken by consensus and deliberation. All interested parties are invited to take part. People usually search for balance and conciliation.

Considering future prospects

Following up relations through time does not make part, as such, of the negotiation process. Nevertheless, in a longer-term perspective, managing your relations is a key factor of success. In long-term oriented cultures, like Japan, it's even a must! The evolution of the environment (speeding up and digitalisation of information, globalisation, development of emerging countries, etc.) makes the development of networks essential. There are multiple and various methods to maintain these networks. We recommend you to seize opportunities and not to be opportunist (in the flattest sense of the word). Being yourself is essential.

Case studies

Proposal of a long-term approach

ZA

In Saudi Arabia, the rhythm of negotiations is much slower than in Western countries in general. It is recommended to be patient. You should know that many Saudi Arabian are looking for long-term partners, not for mere providers. Putting forward a short-term approach may, in some cases, prove an utterly counter-productive approach. It is recommended to bank on long-term relations by, for example, keeping the same interlocutors.

What are the expected results

DE   MX

Germany has a universalist culture which strongly tends to go by rules and procedures. This type of culture is of a rather abstract nature and discards all exceptions which might weaken the influence of laws. These cultures favour the implementation of rules and procedures in order to guarantee a certain level of coherence and fairness in the system. Therefore, people will rather try and achieve results in line with the rules in force.

In contrast, in countries like Mexico with rather particularist cultures, people tend to favour flexibility and adaptation to local situations. They will rather try and achieve results in line with given situations.

The future approach you are putting forward must reflect everybody's interests!

Conclusion

Each stage of the negotiation process has its own *raison d'être*, which is why each of them should be fully implemented.

Throughout the process, you should:
- bear in mind the objectives and stakes of the negotiation;
- stay within the boundaries of the negotiation;
- try to find a common ground and keep developing it. It is indeed by improving this common ground that the most innovative and suitable solutions are usually found. The cornerstone of common ground is often to be found in the parties' future objectives or in the negotiation process itself;
- establish a common language and draw a difference between misunderstandings and disagreements.

In negotiation, the "rules of the game" must be quickly identified. Negotiation is a question of balance between assertiveness and flexibility. You must be able to support your point of view while always paying attention to the needs and proposals of the other party.

PART 3

SELF-ASSESSMENT AND PUTTING THEORY INTO PRACTICE

"Know yourself and you will know the universe and the gods."
Inscription on the entrance of the temple of Delphi, improved by Socrates

This book invites all negotiators to discover their own style and improve their skills in order to take action! Negotiation is like a living matter. You can work on it and it is a process under constant evolution and redefinition.

CHAPTER 7

ASSESSMENT OF YOUR NEGOTIATING STYLE AND SKILLS

"Self-confidence is no substitute for skills."
Olivier Lockert

Subject: assessing your negotiating skills and style in order to develop your own "trademark" in terms of negotiation.

In absolute terms, there are no good or bad negotiating styles. The most important thing is to be yourself. There is nothing worse than somebody pretending to be something s/he is not. Negotiation (especially intercultural negotiation) is both an art and a science. Developing your abilities and skills is of great importance. Knowing who you are and being able to assess yourself is a major advantage in negotiation.

Characteristics and skills of an experienced international negotiator

A good international negotiator must:
- have knowledge of the cultural, political, economical and social environment (similarities/differences);
- be aware of the various negotiating styles;
- be able to assess the constraints of an organisation, knowing his room for manoeuvre;
- be able to define clear objectives and keep enough room for manoeuvre;
- be able to set priorities;
- be able to examine different options and possibilities;
- identify common interests and conflicts (negotiate, possible compromises);
- use the help available;
- have empathy (the ability to put oneself in somebody else's shoes, understand the way people think, listen and easily establish relations);

- be able to ask appropriate questions and obtain all the necessary information.

An international negotiator must make sure s/he permanently improves the following skills:
- language knowledge;
- general culture;
- self-knowledge;
- open-mindedness and curiosity;
- ability to be attentive;
- time management;
- planning skills;
- mastering the necessary information (whether be it technical, economic, cultural, etc.).

As an international negotiator, you will have to assess your level of abilities and skills according to this list and define the actions to be taken in order to improve your performance and/or status of negotiator.

Assessing your negotiating skills and style

Assessing your negotiating skills

As is the case with all aptitudes, negotiation can be learned, practised and mastered. The questionnaire below will help you identify your strengths as well as the points you should develop as a negotiator.

Table 7.1 – Assessment system

0	1	2	3	4	5
Non-existent					Excellent

Table 7.2 – Assessment chart

	Assessment level					
Skill types	0	1	2	3	4	5
Linguistic level (number of languages spoken / level of knowledge)						
Level of general culture (in several areas: arts, topical subjects, etc.)						
Level of self-knowledge (conscious identification of your ambitions, weaknesses, strengths, etc.)						
Level of open-mindedness and curiosity (regarding new people, technologies, concept, etc.)						
Level of attention (the listening/speaking time ratio can be a first indicator)						
Level of competence in time management						
Level of competence in planning						
Level of information (are you able to get the necessary information on time?)						
Other						

Assessing your negotiating style

▶ **Questionnaire**

Amongst the phrases listed below, choose the one which suits you best.

1. During the preparation stage of the negotiation, which is one of the first things you do?
    a) You wonder about the other party while hoping none of the parties will have the upper hand in the negotiation process.

b) You get mentally prepared to compete with the other party and consider a strategy to that end.

c) You get carefully and thoroughly prepared while trying to strengthen your position.

2. During the first meeting with the other party…

   a) you take the time to socialise and make sure to establish a positive atmosphere before starting the negotiation.

   b) you get directly to the heart of the matter by presenting your objectives, information, etc. Social formalities are reduced to their simplest terms.

   c) you start the negotiation slowly and by listening to the other party before presenting your information and points of view.

3. During the negotiation, when exchanging points of view and information…

   a) you make sure that the other party understands your points and arguments and that s/he knows that his/her opinions are understood and matter to you.

   b) you mainly present pieces of information which might strengthen your position.

   c) you provide a lot of detailed, sequential and complete information because you consider it to be important for the good development of the negotiation.

4. When reaching an agreement on a specific point turns out to be difficult…

   a) you are ready to reconsider your position in order to maintain your relation with the other party.

   b) you tend to stick to your line. The result takes precedence over your relations with the other party.

   c) you ask questions to the other party in order to better understand their position while continuing to present facts and arguments supporting your position.

5. If the other party surprises you with information that is new to you…

   a) you feel betrayed.

   b) you provide new information as well.

   c) you examine the new information in detail and carefully.

6. When looking for solutions, you sometimes...
   a) let the other party determine (or at least influence) the result of the negotiation.
   b) use the other party's weaknesses to your own advantage.
   c) refuse to change your position if you feel the other party is not being ethical.

7. During the negotiation, the way you communicate with the other party is rather...
   a) informal and not necessarily linked to the negotiation.
   b) assertive and directly linked to the negotiation.
   c) careful, reserved and non-emotional.

8. When a negotiation is not favourable to you, you tend to...
   a) get frustrated if you feel the other party is taking the upper hand.
   b) concentrate on the best strategies to achieve the expected result.
   c) concentrate on available facts and data and to look for viable alternatives.

9. When you need more information from the other party, you...
   a) inquire about the other party's perception and make sure s/he is not under pressure or does not feel threatened by too many questions.
   b) ask the other party direct questions about specific points of interest to you.
   c) ask the other party a lot of questions in order to make sure you have accurate and complete data.

10. When concluding the negotiation...
    a) you pay attention to what the other party thinks of you and make sure to end the negotiation on a positive note.
    b) you are not indifferent to the result of the negotiation and the extent to which they match your expectations.
    c) you pay attention to the other party's opinion and hope s/he feels that the final result of the negotiation is fair.

▶ **Assessing the results of the questionnaire**

Table 7.3

A Majority of A answers	A Majority of B answers	A Majority of C answers
You are a relations-oriented negotiator	You are a results-oriented negotiator	You are a data-oriented negotiator

▶ **Relations-oriented negotiator profile**

This type of negotiators strongly needs recognition, which materialises through partnership. A relations-oriented negotiator:
- attaches importance to relations;
- focuses on feelings and facts;
- feels the need to be appreciated;
- asks a lot of questions;
- gives the impression of not being solely focused on the subject of the negotiation;
- also negotiates with the purpose of building relations;
- often proves to be trustworthy and attentive to others;
- shares the good and not so good things;
- works at a steady pace but does not like pressure;
- seeks harmony.

▶ **Results-oriented negotiator profile**

This type of negotiator first focuses on the substance of the negotiation as well as the expected results. A results-oriented negotiator:
- gives priority to results. Achieving results takes precedence over relations;
- focuses more on facts and less on feelings;
- feels a strong need to win;
- processes information quickly and usually needs few explanations or additional details;
- is often impatient;
- may consider the other party as an opponent;
- is self-confident and assertive;
- may sometimes seem dominant, even aggressive.

▸ **Data-oriented negotiator profile**

Negotiators of this type usually examine all the options (or at least several options) methodically and try to achieve reasonable and fair results. A data-oriented negotiator:
- strongly needs detailed, accurate and measured facts in time during the negotiation;
- does not like to personal feelings to interfere with the negotiation;
- processes information at a slow pace;
- asks a lot of questions;
- is logical, Cartesian and organised;
- may sometimes seem sensitive to other people's feelings;
- is reasonable and organised;
- often talks in a slow and straightforward way:
- is careful;
- is details-oriented.

▸ **Meaning of the average score**

No style is better than another. Experienced negotiators identify their favourite style and the one of the other party(ies). People tend naturally to choose the style they deem best.

In order to efficiently conduct a negotiation and achieve results, being able to identify the other party's favourite negotiating style and to adapt your own accordingly is of fundamental importance.

▸ **Classification of styles**

On the basis of this questionnaire, you can also position yourself according to the spectrum in figure 7.1, depending on whether your style is rather collaborative or competitive.

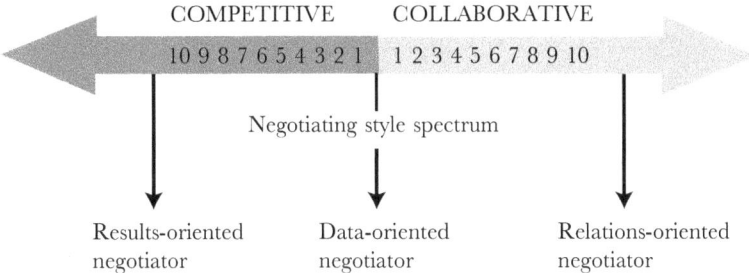

Figure 7.1 – Spectrum representing the negotiating style and the type of negotiator associated with each style

Conclusion

A good international negotiator has varied knowledge and skills, so developing these points is of fundamental importance. Nevertheless, in a few words, an international negotiator needs to be agile, open-minded, able to learn quickly and to call himself into question whenever necessary. There is no panacea. In international negotiation, you must display creativity and ingenuity. In this area, man prevails over the machine.

CHAPTER 8

INTEGRATION SCENARIO

"Nothing is so contagious as an example."
François de la Rochefoucauld

Each case is unique. The method put forward must be considered in a modular way. The patterns are markedly different depending on whether you are dealing with a conflictive negotiation process, an association, etc. The most important is to keep an overview of the situation, identify the key elements and be both flexible and agile in your interactions.

Case study: Establishment of an industrial consortium with the support of the European Community

General context

The case considered takes place over more than 5 years and portrays many exchanges and "pre-negotiation" sessions. We shall focus on the fourth stage: the establishment of the consortium. The three previous stages are relevant in the sense that they specify the setting up of the framework and the understanding of the case.

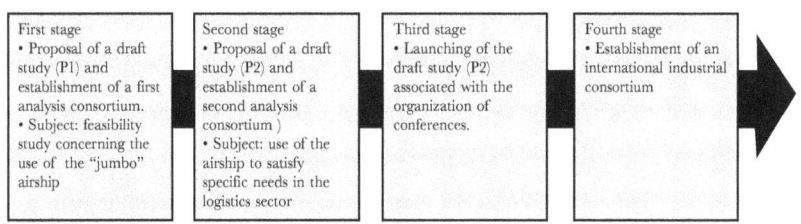

Figure 8.1 – General context
(case study: establishment of an industrial consortium)

Individuals coming from very different environments and cultures interact with each other. The project was coordinated by a French consultancy firm... In a way, as you will find out below, it is a "David and Goliath" story showing how the smallest of partners can remain in an association by adopting an efficient negotiation strategy, which capitalises on the participants' cultural features.

▶ **First stage: proposal of a draft feasibility study on the use of the "jumbo" airship and establishment of a first analysis consortium**

Originally, in February 2004, a French company holding a patent on gas compression techniques contacted the ANVAR (the French State Technology Transfer Agency) with the purpose of launching a feasibility study on the use of jumbo airships.

Thanks to the support of a consultancy firm, the patent holder company established an analysis consortium made up of partners from different backgrounds. A financing proposal for a project worth 2 million Euros is submitted to the European Community.

In July 2004, the financing proposal is rejected. In order to understand why the proposal was turned down, the consortium partners decide to perform an analysis of the situation. In the late 2000's, a development project of jumbo airships was launched by a private consortium. At the time, the project didn't come to anything, apparently because of technological choices and the project orientation (mainly on the national level).

In late July 2004, the analysis consortium partners turn to the French authorities in order to consider new ways of development. A meeting is organised with the participation of all the partners as well as several French institutional investors capable of financing the project or at least of contributing to it. An aeronautical company taking part in the meeting brings out a major logistics problem it is facing and asks the analysis consortium for its opinion on the issue. The size of satellites has been constantly increasing. One day, the transportation of these gigantic industrial products from the factory to the airport will be hugely problematic. This discussion leads some participants to the meeting concerning the financing to change their position. These new members decide to return to the European Community and to reposition their draft study: how could the airship be used in terms of logistics in order to resolve, among other things, problems linked to the transportation of oversized and/or extremely heavy industrial material?

▸ **Second stage: proposal of a draft study on the use of the airship to satisfy specific needs in the logistics sector and establishment of a second analysis consortium.**

In late 2004, a second analysis consortium is established. It is made up of:
- an airship pilot;
- a Russian airship manufacturer;
- the consultancy firm which started the initial project;
- a French lifting company.

In early 2005, the European Community approves a draft study associated with the organisation of conferences in this sector.

▸ **Third stage: launching of the draft study (P2) associated with the organisation of conferences**

Once the project is approved, each partner of the consortium gets to work. Everyone's task is well defined:
- The lifting company must determine how the satellites (and other oversized industrial products) will be transported. The company carries out an evaluation concerning lifting, size and containers. On this basis, it describes the technical specifications of airship transportation;
- The pilot provides a computer simulation of a 6,000 km flight with a virtual airship transporting a load of more than 30 tons;
- The Russian airship manufacturer performs a trial flight (with a 4-ton load) and shoots a video;
- The consultancy firm coordinates and organises the conferences. It also carries out an economic feasibility analysis.

All these activities are performed at the same time, with the exception of the elaboration of the technical specifications by the lifting company, which had to take place beforehand.

In 2007 and 2008, five conferences were organised:
- First conference: the conference took place in France. The objective was to determine how to transport oversized materials (in terms of weight and/or dimensions) in the aeronautical industry;
- Second conference: the conference took place in Russia. The objective was similar to the one of the first meeting, but emphasis was laid on the energy sector;
- Third conference: the conference took place in China. The objective was to consider the use of the airship in the telecommunications industry and in the area of natural disaster management;

- Fourth conference: the conference took place in Brazil. The objective was to promote the use of the airship in the logistics sector in Brazil;
- Fifth conference: the conference took place in Germany. The objective was similar to the one of the conference that took place in Rio de Janeiro.

Many conclusions can be drawn from these conferences:

- The aeronautical industry seems interested in the use of the airship in the logistics sector, but airworthiness certifications are a precondition to any further development;
- The energy sector, and more particularly the oil sector, seems interested to go further;
- The use of the airship in the telecommunications industry and in the area of natural disasters management clearly arouses interest, but this point needs to be further developed.

▸ **Fourth stage: establishment of an international industrial consortium**

An international industrial consortium was established in 2009. It is made up of:

- two Brazilian representatives;
- two Chinese representatives;
- two Russian representatives;
- two French representatives.

Each partner has an initial role:

- finding the sources of financing (Brazilians);
- each country, with the exception of France, shall establish a subsidiary and an airship manufacturing site on its territory in order to cover the respective markets (South America, Russia/Europe, Asia);
- providing the initial technology (Russians);
- coordinating the consortium activities and managing research and development (French).

The joint venture company was registered in France. Each country has its own subsidiary (the French company being the "European" subsidiary) each aiming at developing networks of local partners and providing one/several "centre(s)" and maintenance sites in strategic locations.

▸ **Specificity of the negotiation**

In this case there is an alliance or even an association within a project development framework. Each party has specific competences and knows that none of the other parties have the capacity to efficiently manufacture and market "jumbo" airships on their own.

▶ **Negotiation groups**

There are two distinct negotiation groups:
- the FRC group – France/Russia/China;
- the FB group – France/Brazil.

A negotiation never includes all the parties at the same time, even though they are all part of the same project.

▶ **Negotiation rhythm:**

Here are the major stages of the project (establishment of an industrial consortium):
- 2007: draft study as a starting point for the idea of establishing an industrial consortium;
- December 2007: "Moscow conference";
- June 2008: "Rio de Janeiro conference";
- October 2008: "Friedrichshafen conference";
- November 2008: "airship national conference in China";
- February to April 2009: 2nd Friedrichshafen conference, drafting of the industrial consortium statutes.

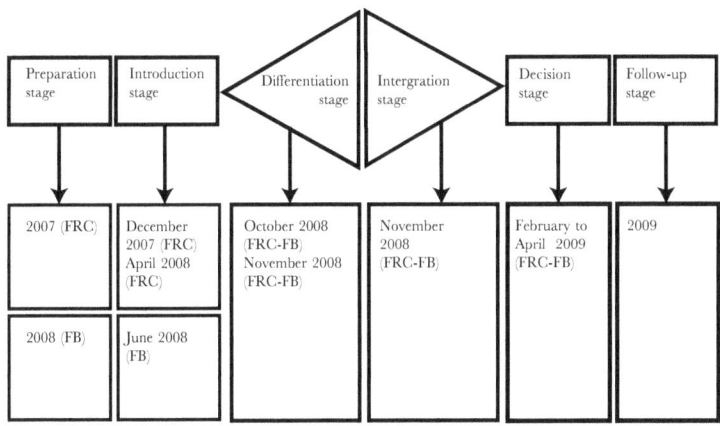

Figure 8.2 – Negotiation stages
(Case study: establishment of an industrial consortium)

▸ **The crux of the negotiation for "David"**

Given that the French, unlike the other partners, do not provide financial resources, the crux of the negotiation for them is to keep a decision power equivalent to the other parties once the consortium has been established.

Preparation of the negotiation

The establishment of an international industrial consortium is the result (as described in the context) of several years of research and development.

▸ **Establishing contact with the participants**

- **Brazil:** the Brazilian representative proactively contacted the French company coordinating the feasibility analysis and the use of the airship in the logistics sector. He got this contact through "the network".
- **China:** the French company got the details of the Chinese participants through the network, via a Chinese friend working for the European Commission.
- **Russia:** the French company also got the details of the Russian participants through the network, via the airship pilot who was an acquaintance of the Russian ambassador.

▸ **Objectives, needs and negotiation threshold**

- *Common objective:* Establishing a strong legal entity in order to support the airship industry development in these different regions.
- *Specific objective:* Each party needs guarantees that they shall not to lose their resources or concerning their relative importance within the consortium in the future.
- *Hidden objective:*
  - for the Russians: participating in a European project in order to earn credibility with their government in order to obtain funds as well as other resources and opportunities;
  - for the Chinese: getting access to the necessary experience and know-how in order to develop the airship industry in China;
  - for the French: being part of an innovative and international association.
- *Common ground:* none of the parties have the ability to achieve the objective on their own, and the group's interests do not go against their national interests. The division of skills and labour is clear.

- *Negotiation threshold:* the French company wishes to establish a system in which it would have a real decision power and a partner status, even though it does not have as much financial resources as the other parties.

▸ **Actual request versus announced request**

In this case, there is no real imbalance between the real and the announced requests. The situation is clear.

▸ **Motives**

- **Brazil:** Affect is considerable. Investing time in interpersonal relations is essential. The Brazilian stakeholder also seems to be keen on, and motivated by, innovation.
- **China:** The notion of security in negotiation is of fundamental importance. In that respect, one of the first meetings with the French consultancy firm will take place in the European Commission.
- **Russia:** The notions of economy and pride are very obvious. "Thinking big" is essential.
- **France:** The notions of innovation and economy are prevailing.

All the parties, possibly with the exception of France, pay a particular attention to the notion of prestige.

▸ **Resources and constraints**

Table 8.1

	Major resource	Major constraint
Brazil	Funds	Know-how
China	Market	Know-how
Russia	Technology	Credibility
France	Know-how and ability to coordinate	Very limited funds compared to the other parties

▸ **Choice of the negotiating style**

Given the nature of the project, all parties adopt a collaborative style. In some way, they all have the feeling to belong to the same team.

▸ **Major directions of the negotiation strategy**

The strategy chosen by the French company could be compared to "a road trip with stops along the way". The French company decides to focus on the following objective: creating a legal entity, source of trust, before dealing with fundamental questions. Metaphorically speaking, the idea is to determine your final destination, to set several intermediary stops, to buy a car, to get all the participants in, to buy enough petrol to reach the first stop, etc. This strategy enables you to avoid nipping an initiative in the bud by trying to deal with all issues right from the start. The idea is first and foremost to bring about willingness.

▸ **Common practices in terms of protocol and communication**

Exchanging business cards and using the right titles is essential with both the Russians and the Chinese.

▸ **Habits and customs in terms of entertainment**

In Brazil, as well as in Russia and in China, the notion of entertainment is relevant. In China, just like in Russia, the parties usually don't think twice before choosing good restaurants...

▸ **Organising the meeting**

The chosen venues are always prestigious and must reflect the partners' quality. A rather long time is dedicated to meetings. Negotiations are not "gotten rid of" as soon as possible.

Table 8.2

First contact	China, Brazil, Russia: through network
Objectives and needs	• Common objective: establishing a strong legal entity in order to support the airship industry development in these different regions. • Specific objective: making sure to keep a relative significance within the consortium in the future. • Hidden objective: Russians (participate to a European project in order to earn credibility); Chinese (have access to experience and know-how); French (be part of an innovative and international association). • Common ground: none of the parties have the ability to achieve the objective on their own and the interests of the group are in line with national interests. The division of competences and work is clear.
What and who influences the parties	Brazil: affect and innovation; China: security; Russia: economy and pride; France: innovation and economy. All the parties, possibly with the exception of France, pay particular attention to the notion of prestige.
Common practices in terms of protocol and communication	Exchanging business cards and using the right titles is essential for both the Russians and the Chinese.
Choice of the negotiation style	Collaborative.
Major directions of the negotiation strategy	"road trip with stops along the way" strategy. First and foremost, bringing about willingness.
Habits and customs in terms of entertainment	• In Brazil, as well as in Russia and in China, the notion of entertainment is important. • Importance of abundance.
Organising the meeting	• Prestigious venues. • Flexible agenda.

Conducting the negotiation

▸ **FRC**

• *December 2008: Moscow conference*
The French and the Chinese already know each other. This conference provides the opportunity to develop relations between those two parties and to introduce the Russians to the Chinese partners.

• *April 2008: Beijing conference*
The Beijing conference is a good opportunity for the French, Russian and Chinese partners to deepen their relations and share their views on the future development of the airship industry.

The Chinese partner welcomes the others. The partners are welcomed by participants coming from high-level public and private companies. This conference will last for a while week. This enables all the parties to be available and not to be under significant time constraints. This conference also gives the Chinese partners the opportunity to show their quality and reliability. All aspects of the conference organisation reflect this approach.

These meetings represent the introduction stage of the negotiations.

▸ **FB**

• *June 2008: Rio de Janeiro conference*
This conference gives the French and Brazilian partners the opportunity to introduce themselves and share their views on the development of the airship industry. Very quickly, the partners establish excellent relations and the CEO of the French consultancy firm somewhat becomes the Brazilian partner's spokesman in the framework of the interactions with the FRC group.

• *October 2008: Friedrichshafen conference*
The main part of the negotiation starts here.

A work meeting between the partners is planned during the Friedrichshafen conference.

To the project coordinator's great surprise, the initially "consultative" meeting (with the underlying question: what do we want to do?) quickly becomes more "assertive" (with the following underlying idea: we know where we want to go. How are we going to get there?). The previous meetings seem

8. Integration scenario 217

to have convinced the partners. The project coordinator notices that the Chinese partners have modified their business cards: reference is made to the industrial consortium and a whole team has been set up.

Here are the members of the delegations at this stage:
- Russia: the company CEO, who is also a renowned academic;
- France: the consultancy firm CEO;
- China: the head office deputy director, the foreign affairs manager, a factory manager, a university professor specialised in airships. Two travel operators are also part of the Chinese delegation, which allows them to combine tourism and business;
- Brazil: absent.

The coordinator adapts his approach to the circumstances. The differentiation stage is not over yet. He presents the concept of a company based in Europe. For the participants, the idea is to find the best way of gathering and capitalising on the partners' accumulated knowledge.

Three points have to be considered:
- capital allocation;
- voting rights allocation;
- allocation of profits.

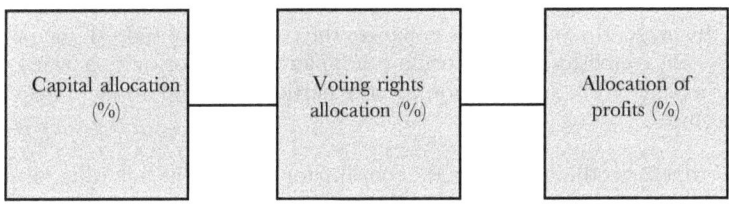

Figure 8.3 – Choice of a legal form to gather and capitalise on the partners' accumulated knowledge
(case study: establishment of an industrial consortium)

Having these points in mind the parties say goodbye and reaffirm their willingness to establish an international consortium together.

- **November 2008: airship national conference in China**

The conference takes place in China in a splendid six-star hotel. The environment is of great importance. The conference lasts three days and a four-hour work session is planned in the agenda. All the parties are away from their workplace. The negotiation takes place in a neutral and pleasant environment: the hotel's private lounge.

For the sake of efficiency, the project coordinator suggests to review a list including tens of practical questions and proceed to vote. This technique allows for quick results and quick identification of the points of agreement, the points of disagreement and the points to further develop. For strategic reasons, some questions were not discussed. The coordinator focused on questions that were essential for the launching of the project.

Some examples of questions:
- Does everybody agree on establishing a joint venture?
- Does everybody agree on establishing a trading company?
- Does everybody agree on being subject to European law?
- Does everybody agree on establishing the head office in France?
- Does everybody agree on granting shares to the company coordinating the project?
- Does everybody agree on allocating voting rights equally and to stick to this ratio in the future?
- etc.

At this stage, the coordinator enhances the common ground. All the parties agree on establishing a joint trading company. Metaphorically speaking, it is like a baby put in an incubator and the parties must find a way to help him develop.

In order to get things moving, the coordinator suggests the following strategy: establish within the consortium a technical branch and a financial branch:
- the technical branch focuses on the development of jumbo airships prototypes meeting the required criteria;
- the financial branch must find the necessary funds for the development of the company.

These two branches are different structures within a complete set.

At this stage, 80% of questions can be put into practice. The coordinator enhances the common ground by reminding the following points:
- The national interests are not in competition with one another;
- Acting within an international organisation is beneficial for all;

- Legal certainty (delivered, amongst others, by the European Community) has a price and it is advised to "share its cost between several participants".

• *From February to April 2009*

The company is established. The parties already enjoy the advantages of participating in an official legal entity. The statutes and the shareholders agreement are reviewed alternately by all the parties. The French communicated them to the Brazilians, who communicated them to the Russians, who communicated them to the Chinese.

At this stage, several questions still need to be discussed, such as the allocation of capital and profits, but the coordinator knows by experience that it is sometimes better to start a project and to consider together how to develop it (by addressing each point in due course) than trying to plan everything from the beginning.

Table 8.4

Start of the negotiation	The parties seek information from their partners
Proposals	• Keep constant voting rights between the four partners (French, Russians, Brazilians and Chinese) • Create a trading company based in the European Community • Creating a technical and a financial branch • All the parties agree on these points. The French capitalise on their long-standing relations with the Chinese team and use this team as an ally in order to convince the other "great powers". In China, alliances are indeed established on a long-term perspective.

Start of the negotiation	The parties seek information from their partners
Common ground, points of agreement and of disagreement	• For the sake of efficiency, the project coordinator suggests to review a list including tens of practical questions and proceed to vote. For strategic reasons, several questions were not discussed. The coordinator focused on questions that were essential for the launching of the project. • Common ground: – the national interests are not in competition with one another; – acting within an international organisation is beneficial for all the parties; – legal certainty (provided, among other things, by the European Community) has a price and it is advised to "share its cost between several participants".
Stakes of the negotiation	• Making sure the common objective is obvious to everybody. • Establishing an international industrial consortium in order to develop the airship industry in different regions (China, Brazil, Europe, Russia). • Ensuring the distinction between the financial and the technical branch. • Making sure that voting rights equally allocated to the parties and that this balance will be maintained. • Avoiding to hold back the project due to initial financial issues. The French adopt a progressive strategy.
Taking a stand	The current and future allocation of voting rights is the major issue on which the French do not want to back down. The French use the following arguments: – their "neutral" position (in a partnership of several "great powers", it is always useful to have a "neutral" small partner); – their knowledge of Europe, its institutions and operation methods (essential point acknowledged by all parties); – their management skills.

Start of the negotiation	The parties seek information from their partners
Taking a stand *(continued)*	The Chinese, acting as faithful allies, are quickly convinced. With their Russian partner, the French are courteous as well as assertive. Given that the fundamental questions were temporarily put aside, this point is accepted.
Are the main problems resolved?	At this stage, for strategic reasons, some points were put aside. The coordinator knows by experience that it is sometimes better to start a project and to consider together how to develop it (by addressing each point in due course) than trying to plan everything from the beginning.
Type of closing	Within the scope of an alliance and given the general atmosphere, it is obvious that the parties conclude the negotiation by themselves.
Methods to start the conclusion	The November 2008 meeting is of crucial importance to this project. Many decisions were taken at that time. The parties met at the private lounge of a six-star hotel looking out over a splendid golf course. The Russian partner is eager to conclude the negotiation in order to enjoy this beautiful golf course. It is a way of motivating the troops.
Implementation	The parties decide to establish the company in early 2009. They already enjoy the advantages of being part of an official legal entity. The statutes and the shareholders agreement are reviewed alternately by all the parties and are later published.
Future prospects	The company is in full development. From now on, each party is going to work on their objectives in the common interest of the group. Future prospects are bright for this long-term partnership.
Power balance	The parties are eager to collaborate. One of the strategies is to put forward skills, qualities, etc. For example, the Chinese do no hesitate to organise a meeting in a splendid six-star hotel. The French call upon the European Community for their first meeting with the Chinese…

Start of the negotiation	The parties seek information from their partners
Negotiation climate	Very good negotiation climate: • time management: the work sessions are integrated to larger conferences. For this reason, the parties are usually more available. The agenda is flexible; • venue management: neutral venues are usually chosen. It is preferable to choose prestigious venues where it is possible to both work and relax. This enables the parties to work longer or, at least, to be ready to get back down to work if necessary; • mood management: the parties make sure to be as clear as possible, especially as they work with interpreters.
Notion of trust	Trust between the parties has been established through time. In this respect, the French made specific efforts in terms of explanations and translations in order to form strong bonds with their Russian partner.
Management of negotiation stages	• The preparation stage started longer ago. The foundations were partially laid through the draft studies described in the context. • The introduction stage took place in several times. It enabled the parties to become well acquainted and, therefore, to get things moving more quickly. • The differentiation stage was carried out more "smoothly". Nevertheless, the major issues were dealt with. • The integration stage lasted less than the introduction stage. • The setting up and follow up stages are now taking place (2009).
Negotiation zone	Focusing first and foremost on the establishment of a legal entity in order to further deal with funding is a way of staying in the negotiation zone.

Start of the negotiation	The parties seek information from their partners
Language adaptation	• For the Brazilians: choice of collaborative words and importance of relations. • For the Russians and the Chinese: use of well-presented supporting documents (use of colours, images, charts, etc.)
Key elements for the negotiating parties	• Brazil (affect and innovation) • China (security) • Russia (economy and pride) • France (innovation and economy). The French know these elements and make sure to have them reflected in their speeches and arguments.

In what way did the French negotiator capitalise on his intercultural negotiation skills?

Mainly through his approach: He launches the project and resolves problems gradually (which is common in China, but rather uncommon in Western countries). He also adapts to a relatively slow negotiation pace.

Through his strategy: He adopts a progressive strategy, which is much more common in China, Russia and Brazil than in the United States or the United Kingdom.

Through the way he communicates and puts forward proposals: For example, he is assertive with the Russians, lays more emphasis on the advantage of having a partner with good knowledge of the European market with the Chinese and focuses on relations with the Brazilians.

Finally, through organisation: choice of venues, times and people.

The airship brings about solutions in the logistics sector. It also lies within the development of greener transport. In that sense, this is a promising. The establishment of this consortium is the living proof that major achievements can be obtained thanks to willingness of a few people.

CHAPTER 9

PRACTICAL FORMS FOR USE DURING NEGOTIATIONS

"Creativity is paying attention to and having respect for the little things in life"
Francesco Alberoni

The forms presented in this chapter are tools aiming at facilitating the negotiation. They shall be of assistance throughout the negotiation process. Filling them in, or at least keeping their titles in mind, shall help you establish your ideas. Like any other tool, it is recommended to use them with flexibility. Therefore, do not hesitate to add a personal touch and further customise them according to your needs if possible!

Form for the preparation of a negotiation

Non-exhaustive list of points to be identified and/or addressed:
- *First contact:* Determine your strategy (method, most appropriate time, follow-up techniques, etc.);
- *Objectives:* determine your basic, realistic and ideal minimum objectives. Also identify the other party's objectives;
- *Negotiation threshold:* once your objectives have been clarified and prioritised, you have to determine the boundaries of the negotiation, i.e. the points beyond which you refuse to go;
- *Announced request versus actual request:* beyond the apparent request, there is the actual request of the parties. You have to understand the reasons behind a request. We are dealing with the notion of need;
- Motives: the idea is to understand what motivates and influences a party's choices;
- *Resources:* what advantages do the parties have?
- *The cost/impact matrix* enables you to classify the other party's advantages, while the cost/risk matrix enables you to visualise your own advantages;
- *Constraints:* which constraints are you supposed to respect?

- *Common ground:* identify the common ground in terms of the process or the future objectives;
- Negotiating style: is it rather competitive or collaborative?
- *Possible strategy:* according to you, which strategy shall the other party adopt?
- *Impact on you:* what will be the consequences of these strategies on you?
- *Actions to be undertaken:* actions you might undertake to react to the other party's actions;
- *The major directions of your negotiation strategy:* determine the number of negotiators involved, their respective roles, the operation methods and internal "rules of procedures", etc;
- *Fallback option:* what is your best alternative?
- *Common practices in terms of protocol and communication:* identify the current codes in terms of greetings, use of titles and forms, gestural codes, offering gifts, dress code, etc.;
- *Habits and customs in terms of entertainment:* identify yours and the other party's (who to invite, where, when, how, why, etc.);
- *Organising the meeting:* determine the organisational points in connection with the agenda (schedule, choice of points in the agenda, possible debate on these issues, etc.), with the venue (your venue, the other party's, another venue, etc.)...

	You	**The other party**
Stakeholders		
First contact		
Objectives		
Negotiation threshold		
Announced request		
Actual request		
Motives		
Resources		
Constraints		
Common ground		
Negotiating style		
Possible strategy		
Impact on you		
Actions to be undertaken (YOU)		

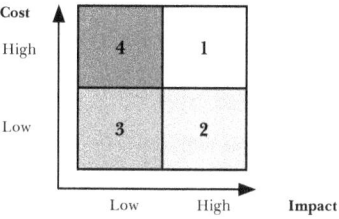 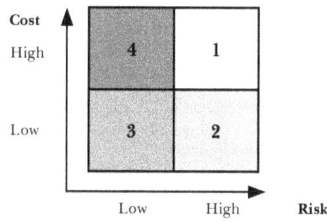

You should also determine the following points as far as *you* are concerned:

The major directions of your strategy	
Your fallback option (BATNA)	
Common practices in terms of protocol and communication	
Habits and customs in terms of entertainment	
Organisation of the meeting	

During the preparation stage, the following table (overleaf) helps you identify the cultural key elements to be taken into consideration during the negotiation process.

			Cultural details	Relation to time	Rules, values and value orientation	Relation to the individual, actions and decisions;	Relation to space and territory	Organisation	Activity	Relation to uncertainty	Reflection mode	Communication and relation patterns
Impact of culture on the different negotiation stages	Step 1: Prepare negotiation		Choice of negotiators									
			Situation analysis									
			Bases and priorities									
			Strategy and negotiating style									
			First contact and organisation of the meeting									
	Step 2: Conduct the negotiation		Beginning of the negotiation									
			Communication (information, proposals, counter-proposals and positions)									
	Step 3: Close the negotiation and consider future prospects		Decision making and implementation of the agreement									
			Results and future prospects									
	Throughout the negotiation		Rhythm and evolution of the negotiation									
			Persuasion & way of getting the negotiation further									
			Power balance and climate management									
			Notion of trust									

Note: In order to read and especially fill in the tables more easily, it is recommended that you split them when using them in the field.

Form for the conduct of the negotiation

Non-exhaustive list of points to be identified and/or addressed:
- Beginning of the negotiation: identify the usual greeting, the importance of socialising, the way to start the negotiation, the messages emphasised…;
- actual request;
- group dynamics: You have to identify the elements linking and separating the members of the other group;
- your initial proposals;
- the other party's initial proposals;
- the other party's proposals and reactions (follow-up);
- your counter-proposals and reactions (follow-up).

It is essential to keep up with the following exchanges:

- **common** ground;
- points of disagreement;
- points of agreement;
- your stand;
- the other party's stand.

Beginning of the negotiation	
Actual request	
Group dynamics	
Your initial proposals	
The other party's initial proposals	
The other party's proposals and reactions (follow-up)	
Your counter-proposals and reactions (follow-up)	
Common ground	
Points of disagreement	
Points of agreement	
Your stand	
The other party's stand	

At this stage, it is recommended to keep your preparatory notes within reach, confirm them, invalidate them and complete them if necessary.

Form for the closing of the negotiation and future prospects

Non-exhaustive list of points to be identified and/or addressed:
- type of closing: will you close the negotiation by yourself or with the support of third parties (mediator or arbitrator)?
- have the major problems been resolved?
- methods to start the conclusion of the negotiation;
- reactions of the other party;
- your last bid;
- last offer of the other party;
- methods to encourage the other party to close the negotiation;
- reaction of the other party;
- implementation: – define the implementation plan, the means of implementation in case of delay or any other problem...;
- future prospects.

Type of closing	
Have the major problems been resolved?	
Methods to start the conclusion of the negotiation	
Reactions of the other party	
Your last bid	
Last offer of the other party	
Methods to encourage the other party to close the negotiation	
Reaction of the other party	
Implementation	
Future prospects	

Form to be used throughout the negotiation

Non-exhaustive list of points to be identified and/or addressed:
- stakes of the negotiation;
- power balance: perform a general assessment;
- identification of the other party's tactics: are these tactics collaborative or are they competitive?
- your tactics to restore power balance: the same distinction can be drawn;
- negotiation climate: perform a general assessment as well;
- time management: do you favour blue collaborative signals or red competitive signals?
- space management: the same distinction can be drawn. Examine the decoration, furniture, surroundings, seats arrangement, equipment, personal comfort, personal presentation, etc;
- mood management: using such elements as spoken language, voice tone and rhythm, language structure, ability to listen, etc;
- notion of trust: assessing trust and trying to turn it into previsibility;
- reaction of the other party;
- management of the negotiation stages: determine the current stage (preparation, introduction, differentiation, integration, setting up or follow-up) and whether all the stages have been fully completed.
- negotiation zone: perform a general assessment; identify the boundaries of the negotiation zone as well as potential techniques to break the deadlock and observe the other party's reaction;
- language adaptation: check if your messages have been well received and understood; identify the elements of noise and the other party's reactions;
- major key elements for the other parties (cf. CASEPriN): regarding comfort, affection, security, economy, pride, novelty...;
- using the power of listening and of asking questions: assessment;
- sources of blockage;
- asking questions: why do you ask questions? Why does the other party ask questions? Assess the other party's reactions towards the technique of asking questions;
- formulating answers: your answers and the other party's;
- use of silence: by you and the other party.

	Time 1	Time 2	Time 3
Stakes of the negotiation			
Power balance			
Identification of the other party's tactics			
Your tactics to restore power balance			
Negotiation climate			
Time management			
Space management			
Mood management			
Notion of trust			
Reaction of the other party			
Management of the negotiation stages			
Negotiation zone			
Language adaptation			
Major key elements for the negotiating parties			
Using the power of listening and of asking questions			
Sources of blockage			
Asking questions			
Formulating answers			
Use of silence			

The aim is to use this table as a barometer. In this respect, the listed information should be concise.

BIBLIOGRAPHY

ADLER N., *International dimensions of organizational behavior*, South Western, 2002.

ANDRE S., *Le secret des orateurs*, Editions Strategies, 2002.

BARNEY J. B., *Gaining and sustaining competitive advantage*, Prentice Hall, 2001.

BAZERMAN M. H. and NEALE M. A., *Negotiating Rationally*, The Free Press, 1992.

BELLENGER L., *Les fondamentaux de la negociation*, ESF Editeur, 2004.

BOLLINGER D. and HOFSTEDE G., *Cultural constraints in management theories*, 1993.

BOURRELLY R., *Methodes et astuces pour mieux negocier*, Editions d'Organisation, 2007.

CAMERON K.S. and QUINN R.E., *Diagnosing and Changing Organizational Culture:Based on the Competing Values Framework*, Prentice Hall, 1999.

CAVUSGIL S., GHAURI P. and AGARWAL M., *Doing business in emerging markets: entry and negotiation strategies*, Sage Publications, 2002.

DRESSER N., *Multicultural manners*, John Wiley & Sons, 2005.

FISHER R. and URY W., *Getting to Yes, How to Negotiate Agreement without Giving In*, Penguin Books, 1991.

GESTELAND R., *Cross cultural business behavior. Marketing, negotiating and managing across cultures*, Copenhagen Business School Press, 1999.

GHAURI P. and USUNIER J.C., *International business negotiations*, Pergamon, 1996.

GUEGUEN N., *Cent petites experiences en psychologie du consommateur*, Dunod, 2005.

HALL E.T., *The dance of life*, Anchor Press, 1983.

HALL E.T., *Beyond culture*, Anchor Press Doubleday, 1976.

HALL E.T., *The hidden dimension*, Anchor Press Doubleday, 1966.

HAMPDEN-TURNER C. and TROMPENAARS F., *The seven cultures of capitalism*, Currency/Doubleday, 1993.

HINDLE T., *Parler en public*, Dorling Kindersley Limited, 1998.

HOFSTEDE G. J., PEDERSEN P. B. and HOFSTEDE G., *Exploring culture*, Nicholas Brealey Publishing, 2002.

HOFSTEDE G. and HOFSTEDE G.J., *Cultures and organization: the software of the mind*, McGraw-Hill International, 2004.

HOFSTEDE G., *Culture's consequences*, Sage Publications, 2001.

KOHLRIESER G., *Negociations sensibles*, Pearson Education France, 2007.

LE BRAS F., *L'heure pour convaincre en entretien*, Marabout, 2009.

LEE C., *The new rules of international negotiation*, Career Press, 2007.

LEWICKI R. J., LITTERER J. A., MINTON J. W., SAUNDERS D. M., *Negotiation*, Richard D. Irwin Inc, 1994.

LEWIS R.D., *When cultures collide. Leading across cultures*, Nicholas Brealey International, 2006.

MORRISON T. and CONAWAY W.A., *Kiss, bow or shake hands: Asia*, Adams Media, 2007.

MORRISON T. and CONAWAY W.A., *Kiss, bow or shake hands: Latin America*, Adams Media, 2007.

MORRISON T. and CONAWAY W.A., *Kiss, bow or shake hands: Europe*, Adams Media, 2007.

MORRISON T. and CONAWAY W.A., *Kiss, bow or shake hands*, Adams Media, 2006.

NIERENBERG G., *Tout pour reussir*, Editions Albin Michel, 1986 (edition originale americaine Fundamentals of negotiating, 1968, 1971, 1973).

PETERSON B., *Cultural intelligence*, Nicholas Brealey Publishing, 2004.

ROMAIN C., *Bien negocier, toutes les techniques pour bien negocier au quotidien*, Marabout, 2007.

ROSINSKI P., *Coaching across cultures*, Nicholas Brealey Publishing, 2003.

SHANNON C.E. and WEAVER W., *A Mathematical Theory of Communication*, University of Illinois Press, 1949.

TAYEB M., *International business. Theories, policies and practices*, Prentice Hall, 2000.

TLATLI F. and HOLSCHUH M., *Successful Marketing in Emerging Markets*, Gestion2000, 2008.

TROMPENAARS F. and HAMPDEN-TURNER C., *Riding the waves of culture*, McGraw Hill, 1998.

WEISS S., "Negotiating with Romans", *Sloan Management Review*, 1994.

WONG Y. H. and LEUNG T. K. P., *Guanxi, relationship marketing in a chinese context*, International Business Press, 2001.

INDEX OF IDEAS

A
Arbitration 191

B
BATNA/MESORE 87
Be-er 33

C
CASEPriN 122
Collaborative 98, 205
Common assumptions 23
Common ground 82, 118, 119
Communication model 93
    Shannon & Weaver adapted 94
    Shannon & Weaver initial 93
Competitive 71, 98, 205
Context 38
Cooperative 71
Culture 21, 24, 39, 45
    organisational 168, 169

D
Do-er 33

E
Ethnocentricism 26

F
Fundamental variables of negotiation 57

G
"Glocal" approach 28
Guanxi 106

I
Iceberg theory 22
Ideology 24
Intercultural GPS 29, 38, 49

M
Managerial logic 35
Mediator 190
Monochronism 31

N
Needs 118, 119
Negotiation 18, 20
    intercultural 18
    international 18, 53
Negotiation climate 71, 74, 75
Negotiation threshold 117
Negotiators 137, 144

P
Parties to the negotiation 107, 163
Polychronism 31
Power 60
Process of negotiation 19

R
Requests
    of the other party 162
    real 160, 161
Rules 23, 32

S

SNA 52, 55, 59, 103
Stages of negotiation 80
    differentiation 81
    integration 82
    preparation 82
Stereotypes 26

T

Tactics 62, 63, 64, 65, 66, 67, 68,
    89, 90, 91, 174, 175
Tolerance for uncertainty 36

Trump cards 136
Trust 76

V

Value orientation 32
Values 23, 32

INDEX OF COUNTRIES

Argentina 84, 114, 147, 151, 157, 167, 193

Australia 77, 92, 94, 96, 143, 152, 162

Austria 77, 96, 102, 110, 114, 162

Belgium 70, 85, 95, 109, 112, 123, 139, 140, 158, 159, 164, 171, 172

Brazil 84, 92, 110, 152, 166, 193

Canada 77, 94, 96, 141, 167

China 24, 69, 78, 95, 102, 106, 120 123, 138, 145, 146, 148, 149, 151, 157, 158, 159, 164, 171, 172, 173, 180, 182, 189, 192

Cuba 24

Egypt 77, 139, 141, 162

France 79, 102, 111, 113, 115, 121, 123, 146, 148, 149, 157, 171, 172, 173, 182, 192

Germany 80, 85, 96, 107, 111, 114, 123, 138, 149, 158, 164, 166, 178, 192, 193, 195

India 84, 112, 121, 162, 165

Indonesia 79, 132, 145, 150, 160, 164, 180, 189, 193

Italy 94, 113, 157, 158, 159

Japan 70, 78, 110, 112, 115, 121, 131, 138, 141, 157, 160, 162, 192, 193

Mexico 70, 84, 151, 195

Morocco 131

Poland 86, 178

Romania 79, 92, 139, 148

Russia 69, 131, 148, 151, 167, 178, 189

Saudi Arabia 77, 78, 85, 95, 112, 148, 162, 194

South Africa 120

Spain 70, 95, 111, 113, 114, 152, 178

Sweden 77, 85, 92, 95, 107, 112, 114, 121, 140, 149, 192, 193

Thailand 112, 148, 162, 193

Tunisia 131

Turkey 77, 92, 146, 160, 186

Ukraine 69, 92, 115, 148

United Kingdom 77, 85, 94, 96, 110, 113, 131, 141, 157, 167, 192, 193

United States 25, 77, 80, 84, 86, 94, 96, 114, 131, 139, 140, 145, 149, 152, 156, 189, 192

www.ingramcontent.com/pod-product-compliance
Lightning Source LLC
Chambersburg PA
CBHW070643160426
43194CB00009B/1554